D0848469

THE BIBLE
THROUGH STAMPS

Brazil
Day of the Bible

by ORD MATEK

KTAV PUBLISHING HOUSE, INC.

NEW YORK

Library of Congress Cataloging in Publication Data

Matek, Ord.
The Bible through stamps.

1. Postage-stamps—Topics—Bible. I. Title.
HE6183.B5M37   769'.564   73-23126
ISBN 0-87068-397-7

MANUFACTURED IN THE UNITED STATES OF AMERICA

TABLE OF CONTENTS

Pentateuch:

Genesis   1
Exodus 68
Leviticus 86
Numbers 90
Deuteronomy 95

Prophets:

Joshua 109
Judges 110
Samuel, I & II 114
Kings, I & II 126
Isaiah 145
Jeremiah 164
Ezekiel 170
Joel 172
Amos 175
Jonah 176
Micah 180
Nahum 182
Zechariah 185

Writings:

Psalms 187

Proverbs 197

Job 202

Song of Songs 204

Esther 206

Daniel 208

Nehemiah 211

Chronicles 215

Bibliographies 220

Scott Number Index 224

Index 226

Dedicated
To Betsy, my wife, and
to my children, Beth, Deborah, Joel and Michael,
who have each in different ways,
helped complete this project.

INTRODUCTION

THE Bible has been studied and examined from every possible perspective. This book represents yet another dimension of reading the Bible. At first glance it seems unlikely that there could be any connection, however remote, between philately and the Bible. There is a traditional statement of advice, however, that urges study of the Bible, again and again, on the grounds that all things may be found in it. Obviously, then, even stamp collecting may be related to the Bible.

In building a collection of stamps that have biblical content, and in reading the Bible through its appearance on postage stamps from all over the world, it cannot be expected that all areas of the Bible can be evenly covered. This book, therefore, was designed to follow biblical chronology, based on the available stamps, but to retain the freedom to elaborate on each theme in whichever direction seemed most interesting. As such, there is no sequence in the usual sense. Obviously there is no plot, no story line. Yet, it is hoped that the bits and pieces that are brought to the attention of the reader will nonetheless prove interesting. Every attempt has been made to include all known stamps with biblical content issued up to the year 1971 when the manuscript was completed. (An exception to this is the myriad number of stamps showing the dove of peace—over one-hundred different stamps with variations on this theme exist.)

Not unexpectedly, a large number of stamps in this collection come from Israel. One could anticipate that the Land of the Bible and the People of the Book would represent a biblical heritage on their stamps.

THE BEGINNING
OF CREATION

United States: 1969
Apollo 8 Space Flight

*In the beginning God created the
heaven and the earth.*

Genesis 1:1

TO commemorate the historic first manned flight
around the moon in December 1968, the Apollo-8 stamp
pictured a view of the earth as it might be seen from the
moon's orbit. Because of the significance of the occasion,
the astronauts while speeding through space, took turns
reading aloud the first verses of Genesis: "In the beginning, God. . . ."

THE FIRST DAY
OF CREATION

Israel: 1965
Festival Set: "Creation"

And God said: 'Let there be light.'
And there was light. And God
saw the light, that it was good;
and God divided the light from
the darkness. And God called the
light Day, and the darkness He
called Night. And there was
evening and there was morning,
one day.

Genesis 1:3-6

CAPTURED in the text of this stamp and tab is a
fascinating controversy in Bible interpretation. Genesis
tells us that it is only on the fourth day that the "greater
light to rule the day, and the lesser light to rule the
night" (probably the sun and moon) were created.
Whence then the light of this first day? Even the great
astronomer and scientist Halley was intrigued with this
question. He suggested that prior to the creation of the
sun, the nebulae gave sufficient illumination to divide
light from darkness as the earth rotated.

THE SECOND DAY
OF CREATION

Israel: 1965
Festival Set: "Creation"
Rosh Hashana 5725

And God said: 'Let there be a
firmament in the midst of the
waters.' And there was evening
and there was morning, a second
day.

Genesis 1:6, 8

"AND there was evening and there was morning, a second day." From this statement came the deduction that a "daily unit" consists of a night preceeding the day. This is embodied in the Jewish calendar where holidays always begin at sundown rather than dawn. (The Sabbath, for example, begins at dusk Friday night and lasts until sundown on Saturday.) An echo of this thought remains visible in the Christian holidays that also "begin" the night before, as exemplified by Christmas Eve.

THE THIRD DAY
OF CREATION

Israel: 1965
Festival Set: "Creation"
Rosh Hashana 5725

And God said: 'Let the waters
under the heaven be gathered
together unto one place, and let
the dry land appear.' And it was
so.

Genesis 1:9

OTHER ancient civilizations also developed creation myths, some of which are even older than the Bible story. Expectedly, there are some similarities, but more often the differences in mood are more significant than differences of detail. As an example of the similarities is the Assyro-Babylonian mythology that depicts a primeval watery chaos.

> "When in the height, heaven was not yet named,
> And the earth beneath did not bear a name,
> . . . .
> Their waters were mingled together."

The difference is in the savage and even repulsive smashing of warring gods which is at a variance with the sublime feeling of Genesis.

THE FOURTH DAY
OF CREATION

Israel: 1965
Festival Set: "Creation"
Rosh Hashana 5725

*And God made the two great
lights: the greater light to rule the
day, and the lesser light to rule
the night; and the stars.*

Genesis 1:16

THE inconsistency in Genesis of the presence of light on the first day, whereas the sun and moon were created only on the fourth day (page 2) is possibly a result of multiple authorship. This is more clearly seen when one recognizes that Genesis is only one of at least three separate and different Bible descriptions of creation. Unlike the Genesis section where creation is unfolded in a story format like acts in a drama, a poetic representation is found in Psalms 19, and yet another in Proverbs 8:22-31, where wisdom presides at the birth of nature. It follows that there is no uniform and binding Jewish belief in the manner of creation other than the fact of creation.

THE FIFTH DAY
OF CREATION

Israel: 1965
Festival Set: "Creation"
Rosh Hashana 5725

And God said: 'Let the waters swarm with swarms of living creatures, and let fowl fly above the earth in the open firmament of heaven.

Genesis 1:20

THE concept of evolution as stated by Darwin has often been described as being in contradiction to the Bible account of creation. There are those of all faiths who read: "Let the waters swarm with swarms of living creatures, and let fowl fly above the earth" as if it described the actual creation of each species. Others, however, find no conflict between evolution and Genesis. They point out that the Bible account moves from lowest to highest and from simplest to most complex. They cite as further evidence that when God decides to give man "dominion" over the other creatures, the Hebrew word can be translated either as "dominion" or "descent."

THE SIXTH DAY
OF CREATION

Israel: 1965
Festival Set: "Creation"
Rosh Hashana 5725

*And God said: 'Let us make man
in our image, after our likeness.'*

Genesis 1:26

VARIOUS interpretations have been given to the use of the plural, "Let *us* make man in *our* image." One explanation is that the plural is a royal first person wherein royal commands are stated in the plural. A more fanciful explanation offered by some scholars suggests God consulted with His angels, and from this we ought to learn to respect our subordinates. Hebrew language scholars, however, offer another interpretation by pointing out that "Let *us* make man" is the idiomatic way of expressing deliberation or a thoughtful process.

GOD CREATES MAN

*And God created man in His
own image, in the image of
God created He him . . . .*

Genesis 1:27

To understand the earth itself better and the global phenomena that characterize it, the International Geophysical Year was established. Research and measurements dealing with aurora, cosmic rays, geomagnetism, glaciology, and seismology (as well as many other fields) were undertaken. It was a worldwide project which began July 1, 1957, and continued for eighteen months. More than forty nations participated in this monumental effort to learn more about man's physical environment. The design of the United States stamp honoring this undertaking shows a tiny detail from a fresco on the ceiling of the Sistine Chapel painted by the famous Michelangelo which depicts God creating man.

ADAM AND EVE

. . . male and female created He them. And God blessed them; and God said unto them: 'Be fruitful, and multiply, and replenish the earth, . . .'
Genesis 1:27-28

THESE stamps are part of a group of stamps issued by Italy honoring the artist Michelangelo, who stands forever as one of the greatest creators in the history of art. The figures of Adam and Eve as well as the other biblical characters shown on the other stamps of this set were all reproduced from the beautiful and extensive work that Michelangelo created on the ceiling of the Sistine Chapel. His full name was Michelangelo Buonarroti; and as little known as his family name is the fact that his genius was expressed as an architect, poet and military engineer as well as painter and sculptor. He was born in 1475 and lived for eighty-nine years, enjoying a rich full life, contradicting the notion that truly great artists have to suffer.

MAN BECOMES A
LIVING SOUL

Belgium: 1962
Rights of Man
Michelangelo's Adam
Detail from the "Creation"

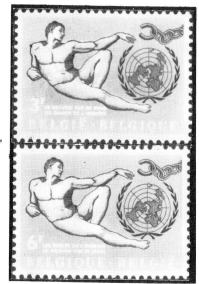

*Then the Lord God formed
man of the dust of the
ground, and breathed into his
nostrils the breath of life;
and man became a living
soul.*
                    Genesis 2:7

THE traditional understanding of this section of the
Bible which details the creation of man after it has
already been described as having taken place in Genesis
I, is that this is not a second creation. Chapter II is
considered as a supplementary explanation of the process
of creation of both man and woman. It is only mentioned in Chapter I as a part of the general scheme of
things. In Chapter II, there is particular emphasis on the
details of the creation of man. Traditionalists of all
faiths build many different implications out of these circumstances, but the general belief is that Man is the
crown and the goal of creation.

ADAM AND EVE IN
THE GARDEN OF EDEN

Ajman: 1968
"Adam" by Dürer

*And the Lord God planted a
garden eastward, in Eden; and
there He put the man whom He had
formed.*

Genesis 2:8

THE design of Ajman's portrayal of Adam is taken
from the paintings of Albrecht Dürer, whose skill and
art in engraving and woodcut design revolutionized the
methods of his time. He lived from 1471 to 1528 and
was considered the greatest artist in his country (Germany) during the Renaissance. Nüremburg, where he
was born, was famous for its woodcarving and his was
considered the work of a genius in engraving and wood-
cutting. His paintings reflect the introspection of Teutonic
philosophies combined with a strong influence of Italian
Renaissance art. One of eighteen children born to a poor
goldsmith, Dürer became the favorite artist of the Emperor Maximilian I and was famous in his own day.

THE TREE OF LIFE

Yemen 1970
Save the Holy Places
Tree of Life

*And out of the ground made
the Lord God to grow every
tree that is pleasant to the
sight, and good for food; the
tree of life also in the midst
of the garden, and the tree of
the knowledge of good and
evil.*

Genesis 2:9

T HERE is a highly imaginative and quite detailed description of the Tree of Life in a thirteenth-century compilation of rabbinic material called *Jalkut Shimeoni.* Its authorship is generally credited to Rabbi Joshua b. Levi who lived in the third century and who had leanings towards mysticism. He states, "In the center is the Tree of Life, its branches covering the whole of Gan Eden, containing five hundred thousand varieties of fruit all differing in appearance and taste. Above it are the clouds of glory, and it is smitten by the four winds so that its odor is wafted from one end of the world to the other."

This stamp is part of a set that was issued by Yemen and which shows various sites that have religious significance for Moslems (and sometimes other religions as well). Most of the stamps show sites that are defined and recognized today. This stamp with the Tree of Life may be the exception.

THE FIRST MAN—ADAM

Maldive Islands: 1968
Human Rights
"Adam" by Rodin

*And the Lord God said: 'It
is not good that man should
be alone; I will make a help
meet for him.'*

Genesis 2:18

ON December 10, 1948, the United Nations adopted
an unprecedented and unique document: the Universal
Declaration of Human Rights. Twenty years later, the
anniversary of the declaration was declared "Human
Rights Year." To commemorate the occasion, many
countries issued postage stamps carrying the suggested
United Nations designs and/or related designs. The
Maldive Islands appropriately decided to feature the first
human beings, Adam and Eve, on their Human Rights
issue. The Adam design is derived from a sculpture by
the famous Rodin.

13

THE LONELINESS OF ADAM

And the man gave names to all cattle, and to the fowl of the air, and to every beast of the field; but for Adam there was not found a help meet for him.

Vatican: 1970
Michelangelo's Adam
Detail from The "Creation"

Genesis 2:20

T HAT man was created before woman, and woman fashioned of man's rib, could easily have led to a religious philosophy of a superior and inferior sex. In fact there are some who point to such biblical data to confirm their bias that women are inferior. The sages who interpreted the Bible, however, would not permit such inequity. In fact, the interpretation given was that woman was man's other self, not a subordinate. The poetic meaning of coming from his rib is that she is intended to be at his side, as needed. He in turn is to protect her and cherish her as a part of himself.

The Talmud in its commentaries on the position of woman makes a point of her importance by citing the story of a pious man and pious woman who were divorced because they were childless. Both married wicked mates. Whereupon he became wicked as a result of his wife's influence, but the pious woman made the wicked husband righteous.

EVE—
THE FIRST WOMAN

Vatican: 1970
Michelangelo's Eve
Detail from the "Creation"

And the rib, which the Lord God
had taken from the man, made
He a woman, and brought her
unto the man.

Genesis 2:22

IN Arabic folk legends, the creation of mankind is a related but fascinatingly different story! The first human was a double being fashioned of clay, part male and part female and, like Siamese twins, joined at the hips. Ultimately, the one person separated into two people, a man and a woman. This first woman, named Quarim, refused to let man dominate as she was his equal and so she was driven out of Paradise and became Satan's mate.

There is an equivalent folk belief among some Jews, built on a Babylonian myth. In this story, Lilith is the first woman created and Eve is fashioned later. The Bible

15

can be interpreted in a way that permits this belief. The first chapter of Genesis seems to speak of the simultaneous creation of male and female; it is in the second chapter that Eve is born of Adam's rib. It is possible to read into this that there was a First Eve (another of Lilith's seventeen names) who was an unsatisfactory mate and, therefore, replaced. Among those who believed in this Lilith, she was seen as the primary female demon. Her hatred and jealousy of Eve was so great that her major interest lay in destroying all newborn babies and mothers in childbirth. To protect newborn children from her, many Jews surrounded the mother and infant with amulets and charms of various kinds. One amulet was a sheet of paper with all of Lilith's seventeen names inscribed. Another was an amulet with the names of three particular angels. Male babies were protected until circumcision and female infants for much longer. Even today, in some backward communities Lilith is feared.

THE SERPENT IN THE GARDEN OF EDEN

Ajman: 1968
"Adam and Eve
with the Serpent" by
Hugo van der Goes

*Now the serpent was more
subtle than any beast of the
field which the Lord God
had made. And he said unto
the woman: 'Yea, hath God
said: Ye shall not eat of any
tree of the garden?'*

Genesis 3:1

IN this painting by Hugo van der Goes, the serpent is portrayed in near human form. This was probably based on the rabbinic legend that the serpent had powers of speech and powers of intellect greater than other animals. Moreover, until the eighteenth century it was held by some traditionalists that the serpent walked upright until it tempted Eve when it was punished by being reduced to crawling on its belly and eating dust.

The artist Hugo van der Goes was born probably in Ghent about the year 1435. In keeping with his times, his paintings were on religious themes. In his later years, he entered a monastery and continued painting until his death in 1482.

THE
TEMPTATION
OF ADAM
BY EVE

Fujeira: 1970
"Adam and Eve"

And the woman said unto
the serpent: 'Of the fruit of
the trees of the garden we
may eat; . . .'

Genesis 3:2

IN the conversation between Eve and the serpent, Eve
exaggerates God's prohibition regarding the Tree of
Knowledge. Where God had said ". . . Thou shalt not eat
of it; for in the day that thou eatest thereof thou shalt
surely die," Eve added . . . "neither shall ye touch it. . . ."
This enlargement on the truth, said the rabbis, was the
cause of her downfall.

The folk tales "explain" how this happened. While
walking one day behind Eve, the serpent managed to push
her hand against the trunk of the tree. It was easy after
that to convince Eve that since she did not die from
touching the tree, neither would she die from eating its
fruit.

ADAM EATS FROM THE TREE OF KNOWLEDGE

Ajman: 1968
"Adam and Eve"
by Lucas Cranach

And when the woman saw that the tree was good for food, and that it was a delight to the eyes, and that the tree was to be desired to make one wise, she took of the fruit thereof, and did eat; and she gave also unto her husband with her, and he did eat.

Genesis 3:6

AJMAN is one of many obscure sheikdoms on the Arab peninsula that has discovered there is much money to be made in issuing stamps. The profit motive in some countries (among them Ajman) seems to be far more important than the postal considerations. There have been instances where promoters abroad, working in collusion with some governments, have influenced the policies of stamp publishing. There have been rare occasions when a stamp issue has been designed, printed, and sold abroad without any justifying postal usage in the country authorizing its sale. This stamp is part of a group with appeal to collectors of famous works of art on stamps, as well as of collectors of "religion" on stamps. Stamps printed for commercial rather than postal use are called "black blot" issues, and are not listed in the Scott catalogues, with the usual numbers. Instead they are catalogued in Scott's "For The Record" as philatelic (non-postal) labels.

ADAM AND EVE COVER THEIR NAKEDNESS

Poland: 1969
Folk carvings

And the eyes of them both were
opened, and they knew that they
were naked; and they sewed
fig-leaves together, and made
themselves girdles.

Genesis 3:7

HAD man not sinned in taking the fruit of the Tree of Knowledge, would he have enjoyed eternal life? One notes that Adam and Eve were forbidden to eat only of the Tree of Knowledge of good and evil, and no mention was made of the Tree of Life. Scholars are not in agreement as to whether man was born to die, or spoiled his chance to live forever by disobeying God. There are three major possibilities in answer to this question: a) in choosing to sin, man forfeited his immortality; b) man was destined to live only for a short span regardless of his behavior in the Garden of Eden; c) man was born to conditional immortality which, had he not eaten of the Tree of Life, could have become permanent or continued immortality.

20

NO HIDING PLACE
FROM GOD

MICHELANGELO: HEAD OF ADAM

*And the Lord God called
unto the man and said unto
him: 'Where art thou?'*

Genesis 3:9

Ajman: 1970
Michelangelo's Adam
Detail from
"The Creation"

I S God not all-powerful and all-knowing? Why, then, should He ask a question of Adam when He knows the answer? The rabbis faced the issue of God's omniscience by the explanation that the question was asked out of consideration for Adam, so that he could collect his thoughts and recover his equanimity. On a deeper level, they suggest that invariably God's voice speaks out (in the form of conscience within man) whenever one sins.

There are three instances in the Bible of God asking a question of man: The first is following the eating of the forbidden fruit. The second is when God asks Cain who has just slain Abel, "Where is your brother?" (Genesis 4:9). The third occurs when the sorcerer Balaam is on his way to curse the people of Israel, and God asks him, "What men are these with thee?" (Numbers 22:9). All three questions are related to a wrongdoing. Taken out of the specific episode wherein each question is connected to particular events and placed in their own sequence, it is interesting to note these questions pose an ethical and moral issue to each reader of the Bible as to how he conducts his own life. "Where are you?, Where is your brother?, and Who are the people with you?", should be seen as God calling upon each reader of the Bible for an accounting. They face man with responsibility for the welfare of his fellowman and with the responsibility to be part of a moral community. Seen in this light, the genius of the Bible is demonstrated in its ability to be read by the youngest and most naive as a moral tale, or the most sophisticated and intelligent as a profound moral document with dazzling insights.

ADAM BLAMES EVE

Grenada: 1970
"Adam and Eve"
by Titian

*And the man said: 'The
woman whom Thou gavest
to be with me, she gave
me of the tree, and I did eat.'*

Genesis 3:12

GRANTED that the serpent managed to tempt Eve
to eat the forbidden fruit, why need Adam also have followed her example? He was free to refuse to commit a
sin. Folk-story tellers constructed an interesting answer
to this question. The fable states that Eve became panic
stricken after she bit into the apple, for God had said to
do so would mean death. Her concern included the notion that Adam would continue to live and that God
would certainly create another woman to live with him.
Therefore, she ran to Adam and confessed both her sinful
deed and her love for him. Adam thereupon decided that
if she had to die, then he would also. With this in mind,
he ate the forbidden fruit.

This stamp is from a reproduction of a mural in the
Grenada pavillion at the World's Fair in Osaka, Japan,
Expo 1970.

PUNISHMENT
FOR SINNING

Ajman: 1968
"Original Sin"
by Maderuelo

*And the Lord God said unto the woman:
'What is this thou hast done?'
And the woman said: 'The
serpent beguiled me, and
I did eat.'*

Genesis 3:13

THE painting by Maderuelo reproduced on this stamp is entitled "Original Sin." The story of Adam and Eve disobeying God and incurring His anger, is part of the Scriptures of both the Jewish and Christian faiths. They differ, however, in their interpretations of this story. Christians hold that all men are born "in sin" because of the original sin. To find salvation, the individual must accept Christ because man's true nature is essentially corrupting. Jews believe that man is born without sin and is capable of being either good or evil, and that he can find salvation through righteous living.

EVE—THE MOTHER
OF ALL LIVING
THINGS

Maldive Islands: 1968
Human Rights
"Eve" by Rodin

And the man called his wife's name Eve; because she was the mother of all living.

Genesis 3:20

CONSIDERED the greatest French sculptor of his age, Auguste Rodin (1840–1917) was initially rebuffed by his contemporaries. He was more interested in expression and character in a work of art, than in the glibness of a smooth surface. Despite the severe criticism he encountered, he continued to translate nature with a reality and brutal intensity to the end that his influence on sculpture became a major force. His single most noted work is probably "The Thinker." His genius as it is expressed in the figures of Adam and Eve is compelling. The use of these on the Maldive Islands Human Rights stamps was a most appropriate touch.

ADAM AND EVE LEAVE THE GARDEN OF EDEN

Therefore the Lord God sent him forth from the garden of Eden, to till the ground from whence he was taken.

Genesis 3:23

Ajman: 1970
Detail from "Fall and Expulsion" by Michelangelo

ADAM and Eve were commanded not to eat the fruit of the Tree of Knowledge. They could eat the fruit from the Tree of Life (immortality) and all the other fruits; only the Tree of Knowledge was forbidden. One meaningful interpretation explains that unlimited knowledge without obedience to Divine Law is dangerous; that is, unlimited knowledge "unrestrained by considerations of humanity" is sinful.

Legends tell us that the fall of man and the expulsion from Eden saddened all creation. From the lowliest stone to the angels of heaven, and the sun and the stars; all mourned man's fate. Only the moon laughed and was therefore punished, for God, too, was full of pity for Adam and Eve. The moon, too, was therefore doomed to grow old and to have to be born and reborn, again and again.

BANISHMENT FROM THE GARDEN OF EDEN

Togo: 1968
"Fall and Expulsion"
by Michelangelo

*So He drove out the man; and
He placed at the east of the
garden of Eden the cherubim,
and the flaming sword which
turned every way to keep the
way to the tree of life.*

Genesis 3:24

T HE exact description of cherubim is unclear. One authority traces them to an Assyrian origin, building on the Akkadian word *Karibu* (one who prays; an intercessor). These were winged creatures with human faces guarding the entrances to temples and palaces who were authorized to intercede with the gods on behalf of men. Varying imaginative descriptions in the Bible give them different appearances and attribute four faces to them simultaneously, although sometimes fewer, and including a human face as well as that of a lion or an eagle. In another description, they seem to be clouds (which can be any and all shapes. In fact, legend holds that angels can assume one shape or another at will). The Bible is clear, however, that the cherubim, in addition to guarding the way to the Garden of Eden, were also guardians of the holy ark.

GOD RESOLVES TO
PUNISH MAN'S VIOLENCE

Iceland: 1953
Handwritten Bible page

*And God said unto Noah: 'The
end of all flesh is come before
Me, for the earth is filled with
violence through them; and
behold, I will destroy them with
the earth.'*

Genesis: 6:13

IN the library at the University of Copenhagen in Den-
mark is a manuscript known as *Stjorn* which dates back
to the year 1400. This Icelandic stamp shows a section
from that manuscript which is written in Icelandic and
tells the biblical story of the flood. Of further interest is
the fact that the Bible page is illuminated. Illumination
is a particular art form which consists of embellishing a
manuscript with silver, gold, or colors. Sometimes the
ornamentation is only a design; more frequently, it is an
illustration of the story—as it is in this instance.

GOD'S CALL TO NOAH

Israel: 1969
Festival Stamps 5730

*Make thee an ark of gopher
wood; with rooms shalt thou
make the ark, and shalt pitch it
within and without with pitch.*

Genesis 6:14

THE histories and folklore of many ancient peoples
also tell of a flood. Of special interest is the eleventh
tablet of the Babylonian epic of Gilgamesh which often
parallels the Bible story of the flood. In the Gilgamesh
epic Utnapishtim is the name of the major hero; and he,
like Noah, is commanded to build a giant ship. The boat
he builds is a cube 120 cubits high, wide, and long.
Noah's ark, in contrast, is 300 cubits long, 50 cubits
wide, and 30 cubits high. (A cubit is thought to be the
distance from the tip of the middle finger to the elbow.)
Both used pitch to waterproof the vessel.

THE ANIMALS
BOARD THE ARK

*And they went in unto Noah
into the ark, two and two of all
flesh wherein is the breath
of life.*

Genesis 7:15

**Israel: 1969
Festival Stamps 5730**

IN the Babylonian epic, it is the gods in their council who decide to destroy man, but Ea, one of the gods, is determined to protect Utnapishtim—a favorite. As can be seen, the Gilgamesh epic does not convey the moral message of the biblical narrative of Noah who was saved because he was righteous. Utnapishtim takes aboard not only all his family and relations, but also "the seed of all living creatures" and in addition the game of the field and the beasts of the field. He also takes aboard all the boatmen and craftsmen.

A Sumerian version has the hero Xisuthros (or Ziusudra) take aboard his relatives, wife, and children and his close friends and also "living creatures, winged and four-footed." Noah, on the other hand, carried only eight persons: his wife and his three sons and their wives, as well as male and female of every species.

THE WATERS RISE

Israel: 1969
Festival Stamps 5730

*And the waters prevailed, and
increased greatly upon the earth;
and the ark went upon the face
of the waters.*

Genesis 7:18

T HERE is much controversy among scholars as to
where so much water came from. Some hold that the rain
itself, falling for forty days and nights, was the sole
source of the floodwaters. More frequently, tidal waves
and rising subterranean waters resulting from cyclones
and earthquakes are also suggested as being major causes
of the flood. Evidence for this is found in the phrases of
the Bible which state that "on the same day were all the
fountains of the great deep broken up, and the windows of
heaven were opened."

THE ARK COMES TO REST

Armenia: 1920
Mount Ararat

*And the ark rested in the seventh
month on the seventeenth day
upon the mountains of Ararat.*

Genesis 8:4

IN the Gilgamesh epic, it is recorded that Utnapishtim's boat came to rest on Mount Nisir, which means, "Mount of Salvation." The landing place of the boat of Xisuthros, however, has been determined to be in the mountains of Armenia. This is also the location of the landing place of Noah's ark. Mount Ararat measures 17,000 feet above sea level.

NOAH SENDS OUT
THE DOVE

Israel: 1969
Festival Stamps 5730

*And he sent forth a dove from
him, to see if the waters were
abated from off the face of the
ground.*

Genesis 8:8

T HERE is reason to believe the practice of using birds
was an established one among ancient mariners. According to Pliny, birds (often pigeons) were released when a
ship had lost its course. The directions of flight taken by
the birds would help the sailors determine where to look
for land.

THE DOVE RETURNS
WITH AN OLIVE
LEAF

Vatican: 1938

*And the dove came in to
him at eventide, and lo in
her mouth an olive leaf
freshly plucked; so Noah
knew that the waters were
abated from off the earth.*

Genesis 8:11

FOR obvious reasons, the symbol of the dove with the olive branch has held much appeal to men down through the ages, becoming ultimately a symbol of the search for peace. It is a design that has been printed on the stamps of most countries. The rabbis have made much of the fact that it was a bitter olive leaf the dove brought back. They interpret the particulars here to carry the message from the bird to man that it is preferable to have bitter food that comes from God (or with freedom) than the sweetest food at the hand of man.

THE FIRST RAINBOW

Italy: 1953
Fourth Anniversary
of the Atlantic Pact

*I have set My bow in the
cloud, and it shall be for a
token of a covenant between
Me and the earth.*

Genesis 9:13

W HILE there is some dispute about the derivation of
the Hebrew word for covenant (*brit*) all scholars are
agreed that it means more than just a contract. The modern concept of a contract carries with it the sense of obligation to a specific external commitment, whereas covenant implies a pledge of "spiritual loyalty" or "communion of souls" in addition to whatever other agreements are reached. In contrast to the writings of other
ancient peoples, only the Hebrews describe a covenant
between God and man. This covenant between God and
Noah is the first, but the great covenant is made later
with Abraham. Even the Sabbath is described at the time
of Moses as a perpetual covenant sign.

GOD MAKES A COVENANT

*And it shall come to pass,
when I bring clouds over the
earth, and the bow is seen
in the cloud, that I will
remember My covenant,
which is between Me and
you and every living
creature of all flesh; and the
waters shall no more become
a flood to destroy all flesh.*

Genesis 9:14-15

Israel: 1969
Festival Stamps 5730

ACCORDING to Jewish folklore, the story is told of
a stranger who asks why God created man at all, knowing He would later want to destroy him because of his
wickedness. The answer he gets is a question: What were
his feelings when his sons were born? Whereupon he
recalls the pleasure he experienced at the birth of his
children. Another question follows. Did he not then know
they would someday die? He answers: "One should be
happy when it is time to be happy and when the time
comes for grieving, then one should grieve." He thereby
answers the original question. Moreover he is told man is
not ever totally destroyed. The virtue of the righteous re-
deems the wicked. For the sake of good men such as
Noah, and Methuselah, God refrains from totally destroying the world.

THE MEANING OF
THE RAINBOW

Trinidad and Tobago: 1970
25th Anniversary of the U.N.

*And the bow shall be in
the cloud; and I will look
upon it, that I may remember
the everlasting covenant
between God and every
living creature of all flesh
that is upon the earth.*

Genesis: 9:16

AMONG the folk legends that grew around the narrative of Noah and the ark is one that tells of the reactions of the people left behind. While Noah was constructing the ark, they laughed at him. Noah asked them to repent and to change their ways, but they mocked him instead. However, after the ark was completed and loaded these people became frightened. They immediately realized this was no ordinary rain; the rain waters and the waters that were coming up from the deep were boiling hot. At that point several hundred thousand people tried to get aboard the ark. When they could not, they tried to overturn it so that Noah and his family would also die; whereupon wild beasts still on earth attacked them and surrounded the ark to keep it protected from harm. Of course these animals also drowned.

LOT'S WIFE BECOMES
A PILLAR OF SALT

St. Helena: 1934
Lot and Lot's Wife

*But his wife looked back
from behind him, and she
became a pillar of salt.*

Genesis 19:26

T O be converted into a pillar of salt for the small mis-
deed of looking back, seems both an overwhelming penalty and a perverse event contrary to the laws of nature.
The rabbis explain the episode by expanding the defini-
tion of "looking back" to incorporate the idea of lingering
behind. They point out that when Vesuvius erupted at
Pompeii, those who lingered behind were quickly en-
gulfed in the rain of fire and lava. The historian Josephus
claims to have seen the very pillar that once was Lot's
wife. Conceivably the nitrous and saline fallout could en-
crust and preserve a body for a period of time. Folklore
exceeds Josephus's claim by stating that each day cattle
come and lick the pillar of salt—the remains of Lot's wife
and only a small lump remains by nightfall. But in the
morning, the pillar of salt stands again as high as when
Idith was first turned to salt. The claim is that the pillar
stands on the shore of the river Kidron; yet on the tiny
island of St. Helena, far off the coast of Africa, stands
another rock formation named Lot's Wife, probably because its appearance recalled the Bible episode for some-
one.

38

GOD DESTROYS THE CITY OF THE PLAIN

St. Helena: 1934

And it came to pass, when God destroyed the cities of the Plain, that God remembered Abraham, and sent Lot out of the midst of the overthrow, when He overthrew the cities in which Lot dwelt.

Genesis 19:29

PICTURED on this stamp from the island of St. Helena is a map of this British colony. The island is mountainous, rough, and generally not arable. It is of volcanic origin and has perpendicular cliffs 400 to 1000 feet on the east, north, and west sides. It is located some 1200 miles off the coast of Africa and its closest neighbor is the even tinier island of Ascensión, 700 miles away. Despite the inhospitable description this conjures up, the climate is healthful and pleasant. Perhaps this combination of inaccessibility yet with some degree of liveability made it the choice for Napoleon's exile. He was banished to the island in 1815 and lived there, writing his memoirs until his death in 1821. This historical fact is probably St. Helena's major claim to fame.

Of interest are some of the place names discernible on the stamp. In addition to Lot, one can make out the name Man and Horse as well as more mundane places such as The Briars, Plantation, and High Knoll.

ABRAHAM SACRIFICES ISAAC

Yugoslavia: 1970
"Abraham's Sacrifice" by
Federico Benković

And he said: 'Lay not thy hand upon the lad, neither do thou anything unto him; for now I know that thou art a God-fearing man, seeing thou hast not withheld thy son, thine only son, from Me.'

Genesis 22:12

THE amazing story of Abraham's aborted attempt to sacrifice his son Isaac can only be understood properly against the background of the morality of that time. In addition to being a supreme test of Abraham's faith in God (described by some authorities as the tenth and most critical test) it has to be recognized as a determined position against human sacrifice. In those long ago days, human sacrifice, and especially child sacrifice, was the practice among many peoples, including the Egyptians, Aryan and Semitic groups. That Abraham's God refused a human sacrifice had to be more shocking then, than that he demanded one.

In contrast, even at a much later date, and among supposedly more civilized people, the practice of human sacrifice still existed. The nursery rhyme "London bridge is falling down" is a gory reminder of the burial (sometimes alive) of a human being to insure that the gods would not destroy the structure being built. Even as late as the nineteenth century, structures, and especially bridges, were often built on the bones or bodies of people. The Hooghly Bridge over the Ganges River, in India, has a layer of skulls beneath each foundation. It is believed the Halle Bridge, in Germany, is built on the remains of a child. The belief was held that the Aryte Bridge, in Greece, kept falling down until the wife of the mason was walled in alive.

The Jewish understanding of the "binding of Isaac" is that it instructs man to surrender unconditionally to God's will; and that it teaches abhorance of human sacrifice. So important were the moral teachings of this event as seen by the people, that the folktales record that the foundations of the Temple were built out of the bones of the sacrificed ram, and its veins became the strings of King David's harp. Also, that its two horns were made into shofrot, the left horn being the shofar Moses used on Mount Sinai, and the right horn, the shofar which the prophet Elijah will use to announce the Messiah's coming.

REBECCA AT THE WELL

So let it come to pass, that the
damsel to whom I shall say:
Let down thy pitcher, I pray
thee, that I may drink; and she
shall say: Drink, and I will give
thy camels drink also; let the
same be she that Thou hast
appointed for thy servant, even
for Isaac; . . .

Genesis 24:14

ABRAHAM'S servant Eliezer did not know until she identified herself by family that he had found kin to Abraham in his choice of a wife for Isaac. He had established as a test in his mind her consideration of others. In contrast, the folktales tell that the wickedness of the inhabitants of Sodom and Gomorrah came to the attention of heaven because another young girl at a well gave a stranger a drink and was brutally punished for her kindness. The story is that she was taken to an apiary and covered with honey to attract bees to sting her to death. Her death cries were so loud that they pierced heaven so that God determined to destroy the people of Sodom and Gomorrah.

Both Rwandi and Spain have made use of the famous painting by Murillo of *Rebecca at the Well*. Bartolome Estabán Murillo, who lived in the seventeenth century, was one of the foremost artists of Spain. Born of very poor parents, his talent and perseverance enabled him to gain fame and social position. He then married into nobility. He is known as the founder of Academy of Art in Seville as well as for his painting. While he painted primarily religious paintings excelling at saints and madonnas, he is also famous for his portraits of poor street urchins.

REBECCA GIVES WATER TO THE STRANGER

Rwandi: 1967
"Rebecca at the Well"
by Murillo

And she made haste, and let down her pitcher from her shoulder, and said: Drink, and I will give thy camels drink also. So I drank, and she made the camels drink also.

Genesis 24:46

THE meeting of Rachel and Jacob involved an incident at a well, just as did the meeting of Eliezer and Rebecca, Jacob's future wife. In fact, the episode with Rachel and Jacob may have occurred at what is probably the same well. Evidently, to protect the water in the well from becoming polluted or contaminated with sand and dust, the custom in that part of the world was to cover the mouth of the well with a large boulder. This is still done today in some parts of the world.

When Rachel was pointed out to him by the other shepherds, Jacob waited until she came near alone, and he removed the stone from the well. Moving the stone called for an impressive show of strength, since ordinarily the combined efforts of the assembled male shepherds was required to move the stone. Jacob then introduced himself to Rachel and explained that they were cousins.

ISAAC BLESSES JACOB

GOVERT FLINCK 1615 1660 Isaac giving his blessing to Jacob

10 STATE of OMAN

Arabian State of Oman: 1970
"Isaac Blessing Jacob"
by Flinck

Let peoples serve thee,
And nations bow down to
*   thee.*
Be lord over thy brethren,
And let thy mother's son
*   bow down to thee.*
Cursed be every one that
curseth thee,
And blessed be every one
*   that blesseth thee.*

Genesis 27:29

T HE rivalry between the twin brothers Esau and Jacob, is captured in a variety of situations in the Bible itself and in the related folk stories. Even at birth, Jacob is described as holding onto Esau's heel in a vain effort to prevent him from being the first-born. Not succeeding in this attempt, he buys the birth-right of the first-born from Esau and finally tricks his father into blessing him as the first-born (as is depicted in this seventeenth-century painting by Govert Flinck).

Esau is thought by some authorities to be ancestor of the Edomites, who were partly destroyed and partly absorbed by Bedouin tribes. Other authorities feel the Bedouin tribes are direct descendants of Esau. In either event, the reproduction of the painting of Jacob besting Esau and obtaining the coveted blessing is a most curious choice for an Arabian country to issue at this time in history; the Arab countries surrounding Israel are all agreed in their enmity to her.

Perhaps the most intriguing commentary on the strained relationship between twins is to be seen in the many primitive cultures that pose a similar rivalry in their folk myth. Evidently primitive man, in widely diverse parts of the world, held the notion that two children could not be begotten at the same time by one human father. It meant that one of the twins was of divine origin and therefore superior, or of demonic origin and hence inferior to the other.

JACOB DREAMS
OF A LADDER

Yugoslavia: 1970
Issued in connection with
the Day of the Republic . . .
November 29
"Art in Yugoslavia Through the
Centuries—Baroque"
"Jacob's Ladder" by Hristofor
Žefarovic

*And he dreamed, and behold
a ladder set up on the earth,
and the top of it reached to
heaven; and behold the
angels of God ascending and
descending on it.*

Genesis 28:12

THE symbolism and beauty of Jacob's dream has
touched many peoples and provoked many legends. The
coronation chair of England in Westminster Abbey rests
on a large stone known as the Stone of Scone, and also
as the Stone of Destiny. The belief is held by many that
this is, indeed, the same stone upon which Jacob slept,
known as "Jacob's pillow."

A more primitive folktale tells that as Jacob prepared
to settle down for the night, prior to his sleeping and
dreaming of the ladder to heaven, the stones in the vicinity began to quarrel with one another. Each stone
wanted to be the stone of destiny upon which Jacob

would rest his head. Only the intervention of God Himself settled the argument. He willed them all into one large stone which surrounded Jacob like a fortress and protected him from all harm.

Another belief that many people hold is that the very spot where Jacob slept is the place where all the world's prayers go up to heaven, and that, therefore, the stone he slept on was where the Holy of Holies in the Temple was built. The rabbis, however, have taken this story to teach that God is never far off in heaven, but that the earth is full of the glory of God, and that every single place on earth is a gateway to heaven.

JACOB AND HIS FLOCK OF SHEEP

Spain: 1963
"Jacob's Flock"
by Ribera

I will pass through all thy flock
to-day, removing from thence
every speckled and spotted one,
and every dark one among the
sheep, and the spotted and
speckled among the goats; and
of such shall be my hire.

Genesis 30:32

THE sheep in Syria are white and the goats black. According to Jacob's request, he would get as wages only the few mutants that are not true to their usual coloring. He succeeds, it seems, however, in controlling their color by prenatal influence. Interestingly enough, all the traditional commentaries on this section (and even the subsequent contemporary ones seen by this author) seem to accept this interpretation of the verse.

JACOB AND LABAN
MAKE A PACT

*This heap be witness, and the
pillar be witness, that I will not
pass over this heap to thee, and
that thou shalt not pass over this
heap and this pillar unto me,
for harm.*

Genesis 31:52

Surinam: 1968
Commemorates First
Jewish Settlement in
Dutch Guiana

AN unlikely stamp from a little-known country which
refers to an unusual event in the life of the patriarch
Jacob when he was a young man! Pictured on the stamp
is an elaborately detailed grave marker in the Jewish
village (Ioods Dorp) in the country of Surinam in North
America, once Dutch Guiana which has had a well-es-
tablished Jewish community since the fifteenth century.
The Hebrew quotation on the stamp translates, "and this
monument be witness." It refers to the meeting between
Jacob and his father-in-law Laban as they cautiously rec-
onciled following Jacob's flight from his father-in-law's
house with both of his wives, Laban's daughters.

JACOB WRESTLES
THE ANGEL

And Jacob was left alone; and there wrestled a man with him until the breaking of the day.

Genesis 32:25

France: 1963
"Jacob Wrestling
with the Angel"
by Delacroix

GIVEN to painting vivid scenes of action depicted in brilliant colors, the French artist Eugène Delacroix was, by contrast, an extremely introspective man..In his writings he describes himself as slowly changing from a "monster of a child" to a Stoic in philosophy. He was not only an artist but an articulate commentator on the whole human condition.

The painting of *Jacob Wrestling with the Angel* is one of three frescoes Delacroix executed on the walls of the Chapel of the Holy Angels at Saint Sulpice in his native France. Facing it, on the opposite wall is the painting of *Heliodorus Driven from the Temple* and, between the two, the painting of *St. Michael and the Dragon*. Delacroix was chosen as the artist to paint the chapel walls despite his indifference to Christian dogma. In fact, he obtained permission to work even during the worship services on Sundays. The theme of all three of the frescoes at Saint Sulpice deals symbolically with the struggle between good and evil. The artist wrote in his own *Journal* about a year later: "God is within us. He is the inner presence that causes us to admire the beautiful, that makes us glad when we do right, and consoles us for having no share in the happiness of the wicked."

THE ANGEL DOES NOT VANQUISH JACOB

Spain: 1966
"Jacob Wrestling
with the Angel"
by José Sert

And Jacob called the name of the place Peniel: for I have seen God face to face, and my life is preserved.'

Genesis 32:31

T HE scholar Maimonides as well as many other commentators interpret this event as a symbolic outward manifestation of an internal struggle as Jacob wrestles to find himself. Today's psychologists would describe this as an identity crisis. Jacob separates himself from his wives, sons, and goods by sending them on ahead across the river. Alone, he reflects and feels God's presence as he tries to reconcile his baser nature and his nobler ideals. This moment of truth is a reaction to the pending meeting with his brother whom he believes he has reason to fear. Having attained an inner peace, he changes his name from Jacob (the Supplanter—one who wins over his opponents by deceit) to Israel (a champion of God).

THE TOMB OF RACHEL

*And Rachel died, and was buried
in the way to Ephrath—the same
is Bethlehem. And Jacob set up
a pillar upon her grave; the same
is the pillar of Rachel's grave
unto this day.*

Genesis 35:19-20

THE Bible describes Jacob as setting up a pillar in a number of circumstances. The pillar marking Rachel's tomb (which is a holy place in Israel today) was of the kind that was intended as a memorial to "keep one's name alive."

Jacob erected a pillar as witness to his reconciliation with Laban, his father-in-law. The rabbis' interpretation was that building a pillar symbolized that their agreement would stand perpetually. Pillars, then, were erected to commemorate important events (Genesis 31:43).

Following his dream of the ladder to heaven with angels ascending and descending, Jacob set up a pillar, upon awakening, and poured oil upon it to mark the holy site (Genesis 28:16). However, where pagan cults were built around such pillars, as among the Canaanites, the Israelites tore them down (Deuteronomy 16:22).

JOSEPH INTERPRETS A DREAM

And there was with us there a young man, a Hebrew, servant to the captain of the guard; and we told him, and he interpreted to us our dreams; to each man according to his dream he did interpret.

Genesis 41:12

Hungary: 1970
"Joseph Explaining a Dream"
by Giovanni Langetti

W HILE in prison, Joseph correctly predicted the fate of Pharaoh's chief butler and chief baker. He told the butler he would be found innocent by Pharaoh's court, but that the baker would be deemed guilty and hanged. Only this much the Bible tells us, but the folklore explains how Joseph came to his determinations. The folktales provide the reason for both stewards having been imprisoned: The butler was jailed because a fly was found in the king's cup of wine, and the baker because splinters of wood were found in the king's bread. Joseph realized, say the story tellers, that the court could understand that even after a cup was clean, a fly could fall into it after it was filled with wine and being served. However, bread which was kneaded could only have impurities through neglect or a deliberate plan to hurt the king. Armed with this knowledge, Joseph gave a favorable interpretation to the butler's dream and an unfavorable one to the baker's dream.

Israel: 1955
The Twelve Tribes

And Jacob called unto his sons, and said:
'Gather yourselves together,
that I may tell you that
which shall befall you
in the end of days.'

Genesis 49:1

IN 1955, the State of Israel issued a set of twelve stamps featuring the emblems of the tribes of the House of Israel. While the tribes are descendants of the twelve sons of Jacob, there are so many variations in the Bible on this matter, that some scholars have even concluded that perhaps all twelve tribes never existed at exactly the same time. In the blessing of the patriarch Jacob (Genesis 49) twelve sons are mentioned and, by implication, these are the twelve tribes. The blessing of Moses however (Deuteronomy 33) alters the list by omitting Simeon and replacing Joseph with Ephraim and Manasseh. Other biblical tracts have still different arrangements, as the census lists (in Numbers 1:20–43 and Numbers 26:5–50) and the Song of Deborah (Judges 5). The symbols of the twelve tribes therefore vary according to who is doing the interpreting. Moreover, insofar as the blessings of Moses may emphasize a different feature of the same tribe than the blessing of Jacob, a given tribe may be depicted differently. This Israeli set follows the tribes in Jacob's blessing; but some of the emblems are based on the Mosaic blessing.

THE TRIBE OF REUBEN

Israel: 1955

Reuben, thou art my first-born
My might, and the first-fruits of
my strength;
The excellency of dignity, and
the excellency of power.

Genesis 49:3

O F Jacob's twelve sons, Reuben, as the eldest, was entitled by tradition to the hereditary rights of the first-born son. In his blessing, however, Jacob denied him the spiritual meaning of that position, and, in fact, depicted him as "unstable as water" (Genesis 49:4). Jacob's anger stemmed from his discovery that Reuben had been engaged sexually with Jacob's concubine Bilhah (Genesis 35:22). Although this was accepted practice among the peoples of that time, it was infuriating to Jacob. The heir apparent would take possession of his father's wives as an assertion of the right of succession. Jacob never forgave him, however, for his presumption.

The design shows the mandrake plant, which is mentioned in Genesis 30:14 as having been brought back by

Reuben to his mother from the fields. The ancients had many superstitions and beliefs about the mandrake plant, some of which still survive. (The mandrake is the poisonous rootstock of the mayapple.) It was considered an aphrodisiac despite its poisonous potential; it was believed that anyone who pulled it up would be cured of lumbago; that anyone digging it up would be childless. Sometimes the roots resemble a human figure, and the people of old believed that when uprooted the roots gave a demoniacal scream.

THE TRIBE OF SIMEON

SIMEON

יחד
שבטי
ישראל

דברים ל"ג,ה

Israel: 1955

Simeon and Levi are brethren;
Weapons of violence their kinship.

Genesis 49:5

SIMEON is mentioned only in conjunction with Levi in their father's blessing. Moreover, the two, Simeon and Levi, are particularly mentioned as Dinah's brothers (Genesis 34:25 and again, elsewhere, as brothers). However, they are also brothers of Reuben and Judah who are also Jacob's sons by Leah. Therefore, scholars speculated as to why Simeon and Levi in particular were paired. One authority suggested the possibility of a relationship between the twelve tribes and the zodiac—with Simeon and Levi as the twins; Judah represented as a lion; Benjamin shown as a wolf; and Dan depicted as scales. On a more factual note, it is interesting that unlike the other tribes, Simeon's portion in the promised land consisted only of nineteen unconnected cities (Joshua 19:2–9). The tribe of Levi, too, was given no land other than isolated cities, but was dispersed amongst all the other tribes. This was as punishment for their violent revenge perpetrated upon the men of the city of Shechem (Genesis 34) for outrageous behavior with Dinah, their sister.

THE TRIBE
OF JUDAH

*The scepter shall not depart from
 Judah,
Nor the ruler's staff from between
 his feet,
As long as men come to Shiloh;
And unto him shall the obedience
 of the people be.*

Israel: 1955

Genesis 49:10

T HE tribe of Judah carried the leadership in the years
of crossing the desert and during the fighting to conquer
the land of Cannan. No tribe, however, was of pure
descent from one of Jacob's sons. Rather, around the
"nucleus family" others would come, individually and in
small family groups, and included freed slaves, poor relatives from weaker tribes, and even resident foreigners.
In the case of Judah, indications are that the tribe in-
corporated, amongst others, such foreign groups as
Calebites, Canaanites, Edomites, Kenites, Midianites,
and Jerahmeelites, to mention a few.

Judah, whose strength as a tribe grew and waned at
various times, finally became the most powerful, and con-
stituted the Kingdom of Judah. Understandably, its em-

blem was a lion which throughout the Bible is used as a symbol of strength, courage, and majesty. Not only is the lion the most frequently mentioned animal in the Bible (approximately 130 times), but archeological evidence indicates that lions did indeed inhabit biblical Palestine. Christian references to the lion of Judah are not unusual insofar as the Messiah is to be born of the House of King David (which is Judah) and Christ presented such origins.

The lion of Judah has also been given prominence by Ethiopia (Abyssinia), whose royal family claims its ancestry from Menelik I, supposedly the son of King Solomon and the Queen of Sheba.

THE TRIBE OF ZEBULUN

*Zebulun shall dwell at the shore of the sea,
And he shall be a shore for ships,
And his flank shall be upon Zidon.*

Genesis 49:13

Israel: 1955

W HILE Zebulun is strongly associated in the blessings with maritime activity, a careful examination of the boundaries of each tribe seems to indicate no coastal line for Zebulun. Of course, the listed boundaries are hard to follow exactly.

Jacob's twelve sons had four different mothers. Two of these were Jacob's wives and also sisters, Leah and Rachel. The other two were their servants. (Bilhah was Rachel's maid, and Zilpah was Leah's maid.) Polygamy was not immoral among the ancients; it was seen as a meaningful way to continue the lineage through male children. For the same reason concubines were an accepted feature of domestic life. In addition to his concubines, who were considered the property of their master, a man could take several wives. This was especially true of wealthy and important men who could afford to maintain such a household. As the tenth son, born into a household consisting of four families, each with the same father but different mothers, one can only speculate at how complicated life must have been for Zebulun.

THE TRIBE
OF GAD

Israel: 1955

*Gad, a troop shall troop
    upon him;
But he shall troop upon
    their heel.*

Genesis 49:19

GAD
גָּד
גְּד וּד
יְגוּדֶנּוּ

בראשית מ"ט י"ט

T HE tribe of Gad, along with Reuben and part of the tribe of Manasseh, settled east of the Jordan River. To be permitted to do so, they had to promise they would cross the Jordan with the others to win the land from its inhabitants, and then return back across the river to a permanent settlement. That they would do so and return victorious is read by some Bible commentaries into the cryptic sentence that makes up Jacob's blessing of Gad. There is unquestionably a play on words in the statement "a troop shall troop upon him: but he shall troop upon their heel"; yet it does not do justice to the original. The Hebrew consists of only six words, four of which are variations of the sound Gad. In effect that is not only a play on words but alliteration in addition. One writer suggests a translation to read: "A raiding band raids him, but he will band himself against their heel." Even here, while the play on words is obvious, and perhaps the meaning is clearer, the brevity and alliteration are not captured in the translation—and most likely no translation could do any better. Perhaps the following transliteration of the Hebrew text can help give a sense of the alliteration and rhythm. "Gad G'dud ygudenu v'hu yagud akave."

THE TRIBE OF ASHER

Israel: 1955

As for Asher, his bread shall be
  fat,
And he shall yield royal dainties.

Genesis 49:20

A SHER'S name means "happy." Indeed, the tribe enjoyed outstanding prosperity, having been settled in an
exceptionally fertile area. Some Christian scholars speculate that the tribal name comes from a Cannanite deity
Ashera, who was the Cannanite mother-goddess.

65

THE TRIBE OF NATHTALI

Israel: 1955

Naphtali is a hind let loose:
He giveth goodly words.

Genesis 49:21

T HE hind is a female deer, so that a "hind let loose" conveys the idea of graceful motion and swiftness. The goodly words refer to eloquence. So does Jacob bless Naphtali. The daring of Naphtali's men in war is borne out in the Song of Deborah, and repeated biblical passages describe the richness of the tribal lands.

Naphtali was the sixth son born to Jacob, and the second son by Bilhah, Rachel's maid. Unlike Abraham, who drove away Hagar, his concubine, and Ishmael, her son, Jacob seems to accept the sons of his wives and the sons of his concubines as equal. The blessings bestowed on Asher, Gad, Naphtali, and Dan seem to indicate this. To the ancient peoples, sons were a man's riches. That Jacob had twelve sons is an interesting "expected" fact. Twelve was frequently the number in tribal groups, in both biblical geneology and in other sources. Abraham's brother Nahor had twelve sons (Genesis 36:10); Ishmael had twelve sons (Genesis 17:20), as did the tribal groups among the Horites (Genesis 36:20) and the Edomites (Genesis 36:10). Perhaps we are dealing here with a magical or astrological concept. One notes that Joshua, in crossing the Jordan river, had twelve men carry the Holy Ark over the river on twelve stones (Joshua 4:2–3).

THE TRIBE OF BENJAMIN

Israel: 1955

Benjamin is a wolf that raveneth;
In the morning he devoureth the
  prey,
And at even he divideth the spoil.

Genesis 49:27

BENJAMIN

J ACOB'S favorite wife was Rachel, and his youngest
son by her was also the youngest of his twelve sons, and
also his father's favorite. His original name was Ben-oni
(son of my sorrow) because his mother died shortly after
his birth. This was later changed by Jacob to Benjamin
(son of my right hand), which reflected his favored position with his father.

However, Benjamin, the tribal unit, was not so favored
among the other Israelites following an episode at Gibeah.
In fact, all the other tribes rose up against them in war
when the tribe of Benjamin refused to deliver up for
punishment some of the men of Gibeah who had misused
a traveler and his concubine till she died (Judges 19 and
20). Later still they swore an oath that no one of Israel
would give his daughter into marriage to any Benjaminite
(Judges 21). Finally reversing their stand, but not their
vow, they decided not to cut off any tribe of Israel. So
as to not break the vow, the men of Benjamin were encouraged by Israel to catch their wives when the daughters
of Shiloh came out to dance in the vineyards for the annual celebration.

PHARAOH—KING OF EGYPT

United Arab Republic: 1958
"Ramses II"
(the "Pharoah of Oppression")

*Now there arose a new king over
Egypt, who knew not Joseph.*

Exodus 1:8

IT is not possible to say with absolute certainty that this stamp pictures the Pharaoh who oppressed the ancient Hebrews and enslaved them. Egyptian kings took over the monuments left by their predecessors and replaced the names originally on the slabs of stone with their own. There is, however, agreement among scholars that the Hyksos dynasty (originally Bedouin invaders from Arabia) was replaced by descendants of the line it had subdued. The Hebrews were friendly to the Hyksos kings and were an alien people—and, as such, were suspect when "there arose a new king over Egypt who knew not Joseph."

THE TEMPLES OF EGYPT

United Arab Republic: 1963
Save Abu Simbel

*And the Egyptians made the
children of Israel to serve with
rigor. And they made their
lives bitter with hard service, in
mortar and in brick, and in all
manner of service in the field; in
all their service wherein they
made them serve with rigor.*

Exodus 1:13-14

ON the basis of archeological evidence, it appears that
the Abu Simbel temples were built by the slaves of
Ramses II, a large number of whom were the Hebrews
then living in Egypt.

The monument, threatened for centuries by the flooding Nile River, somehow managed to escape damage—
sometimes only by inches. Construction of the Aswan
Dam, however, was certain to cover the giant sandstone

figures for all time. To avert this loss, an international program was initiated at the United Nations to save the monuments before the rising waters made them inaccessible. Suggestions from engineers and others from all over the world were encouraged. Money was also raised in a variety of ways for this seventy-million-dollar project. These stamps were part of the fund raising and publicity.

THE BURNING BUSH

Brazil: 1959
"The Burning Bush"
To Commemorate the
Centennial of Presbyterian
Missionary Efforts

*And an angel of the Lord
appeared unto him in a flame
of fire out of the midst of a
bush; and he looked, and
behold, the bush burned
with fire, and the bush was
not consumed.*

Exodus 3:2

THERE are some Jewish scholars who maintain that the burning bush is properly "a symbol of Israel—small and lowly among the nations, and yet indestructible because of the Divine Spirit that dwelleth within Israel." For all of that, it was chosen by Brazil to commemorate the centennial of Christian Presbyterian efforts. The Divine call on behalf of His people is a message understood by all faiths.

THE GATHERING
OF MANNA

Columbia: 1968
"The Gathering and
Eating of Manna"
by Vasquez
Thirty-ninth Eucharistic
Congress

*And the House of Israel called the
name thereof Manna; and it was
like coriander seed, white; and
the taste of it was like wafers
made with honey.*

Exodus 16:31

T HERE have been many different attempts to explain
Manna, the strange exotic food that was mysteriously provided as the Hebrews became hungry in the desert. It
has been described as edible lichen, or as a sweet juice
exuded from a bush or plant. It has even been described
as the carbohydrate excretia of insects who have fed on
sap of certain plants. The folklore, however, is more interested in how good it tasted than in its origins. It states
that had the people been worthy, they would be living on
manna today. The rabbis held, Manna is "the food of the
age to come."

THE TOMB
OF JETHRO

*Now Jethro, the priest of
Midian, Moses's father-in-
law, heard of all that God
had done for Moses, and for
Israel His people, how that
the Lord had brought Israel
out of Egypt.*

Exodus 18:1

Israel: 1961

THE scene pictured on this Israeli stamp is identified, both in Hebrew and English, as the tomb of Jethro. The father of Moses' wife Zipporah, Jethro was a Midianite priest who gave wise counsel to Moses at various times in his life in Midian. Jethro is also an important historical religious personage to the Druze, who identify him by his Arabic name Nebi Shu'aib. They give homage to him at this shrine near K'far Hittin which is said to be his tomb. Every spring, the greatest festival and pilgrimage of the Druze is held here. The Druze are a unique religious sect deriving from Islam but isolated into a religious community which keeps its sectarian philosophy secret from outsiders—even from those who marry into the group. Of some interest is the fact that the Druze fought on Israel's side against the larger Arab world in 1948 and subsequently.

One of the curiousities of the Bible is the name of Moses' father-in-law. He is not only given the name Jethro (Exodus 18:1), but also identified as Reuel (Exodus 2:18) and as Jeser (Exodus 4:18) as well as Hobab (Numbers 10:29). As a result some scholars cite this as part evidence for the multiple authorship of the Bible.

OPERATION "MAGIC CARPET"

Israel: 1960
World Refugee Year

*Ye have seen what I did
unto the Egyptians, and how
I bore you on eagles' wings,
and brought you
unto myself.*

Exodus 19:4

THE world is aware that an Arab refugee problem exists which was the result of war conditions, in 1948, when Israel became a state. The lack of publicity about Jewish refugees from Arab countries helps the world remain unaware of that problem. The Arab countries, whose vast size and resources would easily permit assimilation of the Arab refugees, prefer to keep them stateless, subsisting on charity in temporary camps, as a propaganda tool against Israel.

The Jews of the world and Israel have, instead, where permitted to do so, resettled the Jewish refugees from Arab countries. "Operation Magic Carpet" was an air rescue project ferrying entire communities of Yemenite Jews from Aden to Israel. Despite the fact that most of them had never seen an airplane, these Oriental Jews willingly boarded, convinced these were the modern "eagles' wings," which would carry them to the promised land.

THE SABBATH DAY

Belgium: 1893
Sabbath Observance

Remember the Sabbath day,
to keep it holy.
Six days shalt thou labor,
and do all the work;
but the seventh day is a Sabbath
unto the Lord thy God,
in it thou shalt not
do any manner of work, . . .

Exodus 20:8-9

THE origins of most festivals that date far back into antiquity are usually obscure. This is true for Sabbath also. Some students of the culture of ancient Babylonia point to some superficial evidence that the Jewish Sabbath developed from such beginnings. (Mostly concerned with the full moon day called *Shabattum,* and with other additional days during the month when it was considered bad luck for royalty, priests, and doctors to carry out their duties.) The majority of scholars, however, are convinced of the unlikelihood of a Babylonian source for the Sabbath. They point up the religious meaning of the day as a day sacred to God, and a day of rest and joy. On the other hand, there is no controversy as to the borrowing of the Sabbath from Judaism by its daughter religions and other later creeds. Christianity of course kept the name Sabbath as well as the meaning, but changed the observance day from Saturday to Sunday. On these stamps the sender could remove or retain the attached tab which instructs (in French and Flemish both) "Do not deliver on Sunday."

THE FIFTH COMMANDMENT

Portugal: 1967
Abolition of the Death Penalty

Thou shalt not murder.

Exodus 20:13

THIS impressive Portuguese stamp commemorating the abolition of the death penalty shows only the one commandment on the stone tablets, almost as though the other nine had disappeared somehow. It brings to mind the folk fable embroidering the events that took place when the Hebrews in the desert made and worshiped an idol while Moses was on Mount Sinai receiving the Decalogue. The story says that "when Moses came down and saw the great multitudes prostrating themselves before the Golden Calf, the tablets in his hands, which up to that moment had been light as a feather, turned as heavy as the dead. He looked up and saw that all the letters on the tablets had flown out, and in his hands remained two blank stones. Moses flung the stones down and they broke when they fell."

THE TEMPLE
MENORAH

*And thou shalt make a
candlestick of pure gold: of
beaten work shall the candlestick
be made . . . And there shall be
six branches going out of the
sides thereof: three branches of
the candlestick out of the one side
thereof, and three branches of
the candlestick out of the other
side thereof . . . And thou shalt
make the lamps thereof, seven; . . .*

Exodus 25:31-38

Israel: 1955
Seventh Anniversary
Independence Day

CHOSEN as one of the ten best stamp designs of 1955
by Great Britain's *Stamp Collectors' Annual,* the menorah
design was described in that periodical as a "curious
combination of the archeological with modern tech-
nique. . . ." Its aesthetic merits are eclipsed however by
its history. The menorah is, since ancient times, the only
authentic Jewish symbol (the six-pointed star of David
notwithstanding!). The Bible authenticates its ancient
usage in the Tabernacle (Exodus 25: 31 to 40) and it is
depicted on the Arch of Titus as a part of the spoils
gathered at the sacking of the Temple in the year 70. The
origin of the symbol is not certain, but at least one writer
(E.R. Goodenough in *Jewish Symbols,* Volume IV,

79

Chapter 4) believes that it is a symbol for a tree. As such it probably had a different base from that represented on the stamp; and, indeed, many archeological artifacts display a tripodlike base, not unlike the roots of a tree (long representative of sprouting life). In the instance of this stamp, the seven-branched candlestick fittingly signifies Israel's Seventh Independence Day.

THE ETERNAL LIGHT

Israel: 1966
5757 Festival Stamp
Eternal Light

*And thou shalt command the
children of Israel, that they bring
unto thee pure olive oil beaten
for the light, to cause a lamp to
burn continually . . . to burn
from evening to morning before
the Lord; it shall be a statute for
ever throughout their generations
on the behalf of the children of
Israel.*

Exodus 27:20-21

IN the ancient Temple in Jerusalem, there stood a seven-branched menorah, each light of which was an oil lamp. While the three lamps on both sides were lit only at night, the central lamp burned always. As a result it came to be named "Perpetual Lamp." The light that is kept burning continuously in all synagogues is derived from this tradition which hallows the biblical injunction, "And thou shalt command the children of Israel . . . to cause a lamp to burn continually. . . ."

MOSES THE LAWGIVER

*And it came to pass, when
Moses came down from
Mount Sinai with the two
tablets of the testimony in
Moses' hand, when he came
down from the mount, that
Moses knew not that the skin
of his face sent forth beams
while He talked with him.*

Exodus 34:29

Paraguay: 1967
Commemorating Epic
National Poem.
"Moses" by Michelangelo

MOSES the lawgiver! Down through the ages, Jewish scholars have emphasized the esteem in which his people held Moses—not only in the biblical past, but also in each successive generation. The Book of Deuteronomy says: "And there hath not arisen a prophet since in Israel like unto Moses, whom the Lord knew face to face. . . ." It is interesting, knowing this, to turn to the folk tales to see another side of the people's understanding of this man. In the fable, Moses is instructed day after day so that he may absorb the wisdom of the universe. But at some point in the instruction, a sea gull, its beak freshly dipped in the sea, comes to rest on the teacher's shoulder. The teacher, who is Elijah, explains, "The gull wishes me to tell you, that knowledge is deeper than the sea, and wisdom greater than all the oceans. Yet your knowledge is as the wetness of its beak compared to the vastness of the ocean. Therefore let no man be proud and say: 'I have learned much and I am wise.' "

THE FACE
OF MOSES

Czechoslovakia: 1964
Sculptures by Michelangelo

*And when Aaron and all the
children of Israel saw Moses,
behold, the skin of his face sent
forth beams; and they were afraid
to come nigh him.*

Exodus 34:30

ON this stamp from Czechoslovakia showing parts of sculptures by Michelangelo, Moses (on the left and rear) is depicted as having horns. This was the result of a misconception held by most people in his day. It came about from a poor translation of the Bible which describes how Moses' face "shone with beams of light," but which was printed in the Latin translation of that time as "sent out horns of light." That an error was made in the translation can be easily understood when one realizes that the Bible is written with no vowels (and in addition the text has no systematic division between words or sentences).

MOSES THE PROPHET

*And the children of Israel
saw the face of Moses, that
the skin of Moses' face sent
forth beams . . .*

Exodus 34:35

State of Upper Yafa
South Arabia: 1970
"Moses" by Michelangelo

GIVEN the error of Christian scholars in translating those sections of the Bible that refer to "beams of light" as "horns of light" it is worth exploring the uses and meanings of the horn in ancient times. Other than its utilitarian purposes of acting as vessels for storing oil and for carrying cosmetics such as eye-paint, the ancient civilizations gave both religious and symbolic meanings to horns. Trumpets were fashioned from horns, and sometimes even used in religious ceremonies, as was the shofar or ram's horn among the Hebrews. Moreover, the traditional shape of the altar was a rectangular block with projections or horns at the upper four corners which were grasped by fugitives seeking asylum. (Other uses or significances of the altar horn are not known.) References in the Bible and in other ancient literatures also indicate that the horn symbolized strength. In the Book of Daniel (7: 8, 8: 21), the reference is to kings and military powers; in I Samuel 2:10 and Ezekiel 29:21, "exalt one's horn" is to strengthen and prosper; and Jeremiah 48:25 describes that to break or cut off his horn is to crush or weaken him. Aside from the interpretations and insights of psychoanalysis, one can appreciate the readiness of the Christian translators to "put" horns on Moses.

CIRCUMCISION

*And in the eighth day the flesh of
his foreskin shall be circumcised.*

Leviticus 12:3

ON this Spanish stamp, Alonso Cana's painting *Circumcision* is reproduced.

The origin of circumcision is not known. However, just as it is not an exclusively Jewish ritual today (at least one-seventh of the world population practices it), so it was not an exclusively Hebrew ritual among the ancients. Present scholarship is generally united in the belief that its beginnings had little to do with health reasons and were most likely connected to the religious notions of primitive man. Evidence of its antiquity is seen in the continued use of a knife of stone in the ritual even when metal knives were available.

Some Bible scholars isolate one style of writing in the Bible and call it the priestly writing. Therein, the history of the world is divided into four periods: ". . . from Adam to Noah; from Noah to Abraham; from Abraham to Moses; and from Moses to the end of the world. In the first period there was no covenant between God and man; therefore God destroyed the world in a flood. The second period was inaugurated by a covenant between God and Noah, the token of which was the rainbow. The third period was inaugurated by a covenant between God and Abraham, the token of which was the circumcision of all males. The fourth period was inaugurated by a covenant with Israel through Moses at Mount Sinai, the token of which was the observance of the Sabbath."

THE GOLDEN RULE

Israel: 1958
United Nations
Human Rights Day

. . . Thou shalt love thy
neighbor as thyself: . . .

Leviticus 19:18

ISRAEL'S Human Rights commemorative is a most remarkable stamp in various ways. The motif "Thou shalt love thy neighbors as thyself" is written in six different languages. (In Hebrew on the stamp, and in the five official languages of the United Nations on the tab at the bottom: Chinese, English, French, Russian, and Spanish). Since all Israeli stamps are printed in the three official languages of the country: Arabic, Hebrew, and English, this is probably the world's record for the number of languages on one stamp. If one recognizes that the word Leviticus, which appears on the tab, is Latin, there are eight languages represented in all.

Chapter 19 of Leviticus occupies the central position of the Pentateuch and verse 18 is at the midpoint of that chapter. This is in keeping with its being regarded as the core of the teachings of the Law. That this Bible chapter is a manual of moral instruction comes, therefore, as no surprise. Understandably, its central idea is the "Golden Rule." The stamp design conveys the antiquity and the divine origin of its message by the use of a stone tablet, and the universality of the message by the use of many languages.

LIBERTY AND FREEDOM

United States: 1926
and
United States: 1965
Liberty Bell

. . . proclaim liberty throughout the land unto all the inhabitants thereof; . . .

Leviticus 25:10

THERE are many interesting bits of data about the Liberty Bell. Inscribed on it is a quotation from Leviticus: "Proclaim liberty throughout all the land unto all the inhabitants thereof." However, the inscription did not refer to the Declaration of Independence, originally. The bell was cast in 1752, at a time when sentiment for an independent America had not yet developed. It became a treasured relic of the struggle for independence and was named Liberty Bell because it was rung July 8, 1776 to call the citizens together for the announcement that the Declaration of Independence had been adopted. It is on permanent display at Independence Hall in Philadelphia, Pennsylvania. The famous crack in the bell dates back to 1835 when it broke while being tolled. However, it was previously cracked while ringing shortly after its arrival from England and was recast in Philadelphia in 1753 from the same metal with the same inscription.

BLOW THE TRUMPET

*Also in the day of your gladness,
and in your appointed seasons,
and in your new moons, ye shall
blow with the trumpets over your
burnt-offerings, and over the
sacrifices of your peace-offerings;
and they shall be to you for a
memorial before your God: I am
the Lord your God.*

Numbers 10:10

Israel: 1955
Festival Stamps

ALTHOUGH few definite facts are certain today regarding musical instruments in biblical times, the use and shape of the ancient trumpet is known. It is mentioned in the Bible fifteen times (not as often as the shofar, or ram's horn, which is mentioned forty times) and the occasions for its use are clearly spelled out. Initially the trumpet was used by watchmen and to give signals at times of war. Later, however, it was used mainly for religious purposes, including the ushering in of the New Year. It is in that connection that it is shown here on this stamp which is one of a series of seven, each depicting a musical instrument of biblical times. The stamps were issued four in one year and three in the next on the occasion of the New Year—high holiday period. The authenticity of its reproduction on the stamp is borne out by the scene in bas relief on the Arch of Titus in Rome which shows spoils of the Temple including trumpets. Again trumpets are also found on coins from the short-lived Bar Cochba period.

THE SPIES RETURN
FROM CANAAN

*And they came into the valley
of Eshkol, and cut down
from thence a branch with
one cluster of grapes, and
they bore it upon a pole
between two; . . .*

Israel 1954
Rosh Hashana: 5715

Numbers 13:23

ONLY two of the twelve scouts that Moses sent to spy
out the land were courageous and convinced that God
would help them win the land. According to the folklore, the other ten described the inhabitants as giants
whose size and strength inspired terror. The proof was
the cluster of grapes, so large that it took eight men to
carry it, (according to the folklore) and one fig and one
pomegranate, so heavy that each required one man to
transport it, that could only point to a people of giants.

In anger God railed at the ten scouts who showed no
faith. (Numbers 14:27) ". . . this evil congregation . . ."
he called them. From this passage, has been deduced
that a Jewish congregation for prayer must consist of a
minimum of ten adult males called a *minyan.*

INTO THE PROMISED LAND

Israel: 1964
Blockade Runners
(Illegal Immigration)

But they presumed to go up to the top of the mountain; nevertheless the ark of the covenant of the Lord, and Moses departed not out of the camp.

Numbers 14:44

T HE choice of a biblical quotation on the tab of this stamp is a decidedly curious one. The obvious correlation is that of "illegal" entry into the Promised Land. The stamp pictures the twentieth-century blockade runners, and the tab refers to the ancient Hebrews who defied God's will and entered the land after He forbade them that privilege. The ancients were attacked and destroyed by the Amalekites and Canaanites when "they presumed to go up" without permission. Surely the designers of the stamp were aware of the Bible incident's conclusion.

Perhaps the tragic ending that befell some of the unsuccessful blockade-running ships justifies the parallel of tab and stamp. Of special note is the ship the *Exodus,* which somehow escaped from Europe loaded beyond capacity with refugees from the Nazi terror. Upon arrival at Haifa, it was rammed by British warships and boarded. The survivors of that "military" action were then deported—to Germany. "They presumed to go up" and were therefore destroyed by the modern counterparts to the Canaanites and the Amalekites.

THE WELL OF MOSES

And Moses lifted up his hand,
and smote the rock with his rod
twice; and water came forth
abundantly, and the congregation
drank, and their cattle.

Numbers 20:11

Switzerland: 1969
National Day (Pro Patria)
A Stained-Glass Window
from the Berne Cathedral

O N this stamp from Switzerland, which is a reproduction of a stained-glass window of the Cathedral of Berne, the artist depicts what he calls "The Children of Israel drinking from the Well of Moses." The so-called "Well of Moses" refers to the flow of water that poured forth from a rock that Moses struck with his staff. There is controversy among Bible scholars, as to precisely how Moses, in following God's instructions to provide water from the rock, somehow sinned. But for their offense, Moses and Aaron were both punished by being excluded from the Promised Land. Some authors claim that their sin was that they expressed doubt that the water would pour forth from a rock. Other writers stress Moses' anger and impatience with the people as an unacceptable attitude. Yet others point out that Moses and Aaron gave the impression that it was not God's work, but that in some mystical fashion it was they who produced the water.

GOD'S CHOSEN PEOPLE

*... Now it is said of Jacob
and of Israel:
'What hath God wrought!'
Behold a people that riseth
up as a lioness,
And as a lion does he lift
himself up; ...*

Numbers 23:23-24

United States: 1944
100th Anniversary of
the Telegraph

IN 1844, when Samuel Morse demonstrated his new invention, the electric telegraph, by sending a message from Baltimore to the chamber of the Supreme Court in Washington, the words he chose for the historic message were, "What hath God wrought!"

The quotation is from the Book of Numbers, Chapter 23. This same phrase appears on the United States stamp commemorating the centennial of the telegram. While the words undoubtedly were meant to give recognition to the fact that scientific discovery is built on unveiling the creations and handiwork of God, they are part of a fascinating Bible story.

Balak, king of Moab frightened by the news of the invincibility of the Israelites who were marching toward his lands, called upon a sorcerer, Balaam, whom he ordered to curse Israel. Time and again Balaam, in attempting to carry out his charge to curse Israel, uttered a blessing instead. One of these "curses" appears in the Jewish Prayer Book, "How goodly are thy tents, O Jacob, Thy dwellings, O Israel." (This same quotation also appears on an Israeli postal cachet under a picture of Weizman, first President of the State of Israel.) "What hath God wrought"—a blessing that began as a curse!

94

A PAGE FROM THE BIBLE

New Zealand: 1968
A Page of Deuteronomy

These are the words which Moses spoke unto all Israel beyond the Jordan; in the wilderness, in the Arabah, over against Suph, between Paran and Tophel, and Laban, and Hazeroth, and Di-zahab.

Deuteronomy 1:1

T HE Bible has been translated into more languages than any other written work. An approximate count of the various tongues and dialects into which the Bible has been printed mounts to over 1400 languages. In some instances the publication of a Bible in a native language was especially difficult because only an oral language existed. The Maori Bible is a case in point.

The task of developing a suitable grammar and vocabulary for the Maori, who had no written language, was performed by the Church Missionary Society at the Bay of Islands. Examples of the difficulties in translating the Bible: in some languages the way a vowel is pronounced determines whether the same sound might mean "this" or "his" or "my"; and the hardness in sounding a consonant might mean the difference between saying "your neighbor's son" versus "your neighbor's ox."

This New Zealand stamp showing the Maori Bible opened to the Book of Deuteronomy was issued to mark the centenary of the publishing of the Bible in Maori in 1868.

95

THE TORAH

And this is the law which Moses set before the children of Israel; . . .

Deuteronomy 4:44

Israel: 1967
Festival Stamps
5728

T he biblical verse which appears on the tab of this stamp from Israel translates as follows: "And this is the law which Moses set before the children of Israel." Whenever the Torah is held aloft during the Jewish worship service, after it has been read from, the congregation recites this verse. In many synagogues additional words are recited to clarify the Divine origin of the Torah. They add, "according to the commandment of the Lord by the hand of Moses."

HEROES OF ISRAEL

*Israel: 1962
Heroes and
Martyrs*

*Hear, O Israel: The Lord our
God, the Lord is one.*

Deuteronomy 6:4

T he Hebrew words on the bottom of this dramatic stamp read, *Yom hashoa vehag'vura*—"Heroes and martyrs day." The reference is to the genocide and the terrifying cruelty to which the Jewish people in Europe were subjected under Hitler and his inhuman Nazi followers in the late 1930s. Six and a half million Jews were systematically killed; many were forced first into slave labor or cruel medical experiments or outright torture; all, however, suffered unthinkable indecencies, were driven from their homes and separated from their families. But even locked into concentration camps and ghettos and isolated from the world, they miraculously forged pockets of rebellion and resistance in attempts to fight off their oppressors and retain their dignity. This unbelievable heroism is also commemorated in this stamp. As a continual memorial, the country of Israel passed a law establishing the twenty-seventh day of the Hebrew month of Nisan as Heroes and Martyrs Day. Each year a stamp set is issued in Israel to recall these events. On this particular stamp the flames are not only symbolic of the fallen, they are formed of the Hebrew words "Sh'ma Yisroel" (Hear, O Israel).

97

THE SEVEN SPECIES

a land of wheat and barley,
and vines and fig trees . . .

Deuteronomy 8:8

"THE seven species!" The pleasure of the newly found bountiful life might tempt the once-slaves to forget the source of plenty as they settled in the fertile land. In this connection the seven species are mentioned as part of the generosity that came, and would continue to come, through a dependency on God. Moses tells the Hebrews what God has done and will continue to do for them provided they follow His laws.

In this light, the choice by the State of Israel of the seven species as the theme of their annual festival stamps to usher in a new year is most interesting. The period around the new year in Judaism is a time for reflection on past behavior with the expectation that it will lead to a return to God.

The stamps themselves are beautifully designed and the attached tabs are also miniature works of art. Each stamp and tab carries the suggestion of the color of the designated fruit of the land. In the text of the tab, which is identical on all seven stamps, the name of the pictured species is shown in its own color and the species is also shown as an illumination in the text. This theme was used for two consecutive years on the festival stamps.

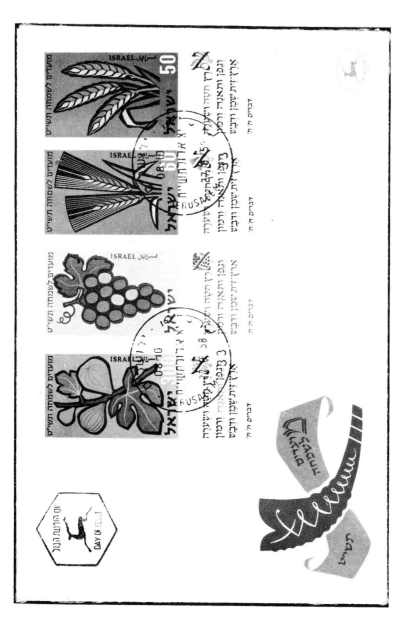

Israel: 1959
Rosh Hashana 5720

A LAND OF FLOWING
MILK AND HONEY

מועדים לשמחה תש"ך

ISRAEL إسرائيل

ישראל 60

אֶרֶץ חִטָּה וּשְׂעֹרָה
וְגֶפֶן וּתְאֵנָה וְרִמּוֹן
אֶרֶץ־זֵית שֶׁמֶן וּדְבָשׁ

דברים ח' ח'

. . . and pomegranates;
a land of olive trees and honey; . . .

Deuteronomy 8:8

Israel 1959
Rosh Hashana 5720

U NLESS the reader is familiar with the fact that Hebrew reads from right to left, he may not recognize that on the two first-day covers pictured here the stamps are in their true order according to the sequence in the quotation (a land of wheat and barley, and vines and fig trees and pomegranates; a land of olive trees and honey).

The illustration for "honey" is a surprise as a cluster of dates is shown. It has a precedent in that some scholars of the Bible, aware that grapes were cultivated as a source of sugar, did not believe that honey from bees was the kind of honey described in the biblical statement, "a land flowing with milk and honey." The juice of grapes flowing from wine presses was reduced by boiling to a sweet liquid called "grape honey."

Israel: 1958
Rosh Hashana 5719

THE PROMISED LAND

Israel: 1950
Illegal Immigration

And the Lord brought us forth
out of Egypt with a mighty hand,
and with an outstretched arm,
and with great terribleness, and
with signs, and with wonders.

Deuteronomy 26:8

UNDER the British mandate, it was not possible for
large numbers of Jews to migrate to Palestine to make
it their home. Even during the height of the Nazi reign
in Europe, when Jews were being annihilated by the
thousands, Britain maintained a vigil on the number of
Jews who could settle in their ancestral land. To circumvent this quota system, illegal immigration in large numbers took place by Jews from all parts of the world. Of
the number who survived the perils of the journey to
Zion, entry into the country itself was hazardous, with
a good possibility of being confined in detention camps
in Cyprus, Mauritius or elsewhere, if caught, as many
were. This stamp depicts symbolically and commemorates the "ingathering of the exiles" as the *aliyah beth* or
illegal immigration was called.

101

THE GATHERING OF THE DISPERSED

אִם־יִהְיֶה נִדַּחֲךָ בִּקְצֵה הַשָּׁמָיִם מִשָּׁם יְקַבֶּצְךָ

DEUTERONOMY 30, 4   דברים ל, ד

Israel: 1964
(First Day Cover)

If any of thine that are dispersed
be in the uttermost parts of heaven,
from thence will the Lord thy God
gather thee, and from thence
will he fetch thee.

Deuteronomy 30:4

INDEED the promise of God to His ancient people that they would be dispersed among the nations (Deuteronomy 30:1), and that they would be gathered subsequently into their own land again, has found fulfillment in our own day. From all over the world Jews have come to make their home in the Promised Land as they continue to build the reality that is the State of Israel.

102

THE ARMY OF ISRAEL

Israel: 1967
Emblem of Zahal, Israel
Defense Force, Commemorating
the Victory in the Six-Day War

And Moses called unto Joshua,
and said unto him in the sight of
all Israel: 'Be strong and of good
courage; for thou shalt go with
this people into the land which
the Lord hath sworn unto their
fathers to give them; and thou
shalt cause them to inherit it.'

Deuteronomy 31:7

IN 1967, when Nasser closed the Straits of Tiran to Israeli ships and succeeded in effecting the removal of the United Nations peace-keeping force, Israel moved against the massed Arab armies on all sides of her. The miracle of the Six Day War where a vastly larger Arab military force was devastated in six days by a determined Israel is the reason for this stamp issue. The stamp pays tribute to the achievements of the Israel Defense Force— Zahal. The design features the emblem of Zahal . . . a sword entwined by the olive branch of peace. The obvious meaning of such an insignia is that even while at war, Israel looks to, and prefers, peace.

THE TRIBE OF LEVI

Israel: 1955

And of Levi he said:
Thy Thummim and Thy Urim be
with Thy holy one,
Whom thou didst prove at
Massah,
With whom Thou didst strive at
the waters of Meribah; . . .

Deuteronomy 33:8

T HE tribe of Levi was allocated no portion of land. Instead it was dispersed among all the other tribes and became the priesthood. Its emblem, the Urim and Thummin about which many scholars differ, is one of the most obscure subjects in the Bible that relate to the priesthood. All are fairly agreed that the words essentially mean "lights" and "perfection." Moreover, the Bible records that the *Urim* and *Thummin* were consulted by the people at critical times to obtain Divine guidance (Numbers 27:21 and I Samuel 28:6). It is unclear whether the breastplate with the precious stones is meant as the

Urim and *Thummin,* or if the breastplate was only a receptacle for it.

Although the breastplate, robe, and skirt are described in minute detail (Exodus 39) as being made of fine twined linen and colored gold, blue, purple, and scarlet, and set with precious stones in four rows of three stones, there is no mention of *Urim* and *Thummin*. Each tribe was represented by a different gem stone. A rabbinical commentary on the Bible from the third century (Midrash Rabba) describes the stones, emblems, and relationship to tribes as clearly as though seen by an eyewitness, although all possible traces of these objects disappeared centuries before. Reuben's stone was ruby; Simeon's, topaz; Levi's, smaragd or emerald; Judah's, carbuncle or red garnet; Issachar's, sapphire; Zebulun's, emerald; Dan's, jacinth or zircon; Gad's, agate; Naphtali's, amethyst; Asher's, beryl; Joseph's, onyx; and Benjamin's jasper.

THE TRIBE OF JOSEPH

Israel: 1955

And of Joseph he said:
Blessed of the Lord be his land;
For the precious things of heaven,
* for the dew,*
And for the deep that coucheth
* beneath, . . .*

Deuteronomy 33:13

J OSEPH was the eleventh son born to Jacob, but he was
the first-born son of Jacob's favorite wife Rachel. The
story of his life shows him to have been a pampered,
spoiled boy and a dreamer who managed in his youth to
alienate his brothers; it shows that later he became a powerful administrator under the Egyptian Pharaoh, whose
authority and generosity kept his brothers alive. His life
story is unfolded in dramatic detail as Joseph replaces
Jacob, his father, as the central figure in the story of the
Hebrews. His two sons Ephraim and Manasseh are singled out by Jacob for a most generous blessing prior to
his death in Egypt. In fact, to this day fathers still incant
over their sons, "God make thee as Ephraim and Manasseh" (Genesis 48:20).

106

THE TRIBE OF ISSACHAR

. . . And, Issacher, in thy tents.
They shall call peoples unto the
  mountain;
There shall they offer sacrifices
  of righteousness;
For they shall suck the
  abundance of the seas,
And the hidden treasures of the
  sand.
                Deuteronomy 33:18-19

ISSACHAR

וּמִבְּנֵי יִשָּׂשכָר
יוֹדְעֵי בִּינָה
לָעִתִּים ..

דברי הימים א י"ב ל"ג

Israel: 1955

UNLIKE the other stamps in the Israeli set of the twelve
tribes, neither the text of Jacob's blessing nor of Moses'
blessing is used in depicting the tribe. Jacob envisages a
beast of burden living in a fertile and pleasant land.
Moses speaks of Issachar, in his tents. The stamp shows
the sun and stars, however. The basis for the design is
the Bible text of I Chronicles 12:32; "And the children
of Issachar, men that had understanding of the times."
Indeed, rabbinical lore tells us that the men of Issachar
were the teachers of Israel. The Talmud views the reference to tents as a quiet stay-at-home life studying the
Law and maintaining a peaceful agricultural existence.

A glimpse into the complications of family life where
polygamy is practiced comes through in the interaction
between Rachel and Leah prior to Issachar's conception.
Rachel asks Leah for some mandrakes that Reuben had
brought from the fields, and Leah retorts that Rachel
has taken away Leah's husband and now wants Leah's
son's mandrakes, as well. Rachel agrees to send Jacob
to Leah in exchange for the mandrakes, and Issachar is
conceived.

THE TRIBE OF DAN

And of Dan he said:
Dan is a lion's whelp,
That leapeth forth from Bashan.

Deuteronomy 33:22

Israel: 1955

T HE tribe of Dan was located in the northernmost region of the land. As such, it was a fighting tribe exposed
to constant harassment by the Amorites and the Philistines. In the wilderness and during the march of Joshua,
the tribe of Dan also held an exposed position at the rear,
striking out in revenge at whomever attacked any strag-
glers. The town of Dan was built at the headwaters of
one of the sources of the Jordan River on the site of
what was once a Sidonian colony. It marked the northern
edge of the Hebrew conquest of Canaan. The expression
"from Dan to Beersheba" aptly described the extent of
that occupation.

As an example of how different the blessing of Jacob is
from the blessing of Moses, compare the quotation from
Deuteronomy 33:22 with Genesis 49:16. (The stamp
design is based on the latter.) "Dan shall judge his people,
as one of the tribes of Israel."

BEYOND THE RIVER

*And Joshua said unto all the
people: 'Thus saith the Lord, the
God of Israel: Your fathers
dwelt of old time beyond the
river, even Terah, the father of
Abraham, and the father of
Nahor; and they served other
gods. . . .'*

Joshua 24:2

Surinam: 1968
Commemorates First
Jewish Settlement in
Dutch Guiana

T HE map shown on this fascinating stamp from Surinam dates back to the seventeenth century. It shows the
Jewish community of about that time, settled on both
sides of the Surinam River. The stamp not only identifies
the location of the synagogue but also notes a section
called *Ioods Dorp* which most likely means Jewtown.
Each individual house is identified by a family name
most of which leave little question of their Jewish origin . . . Benjamin de Costa, Abram de Pina, de Silva,
Elias Ely, Barug de Costa, Parada, Baffelier, Scherpen-
huifer, Nunes de Costa, Schot, Peirson, Isaque Pereim,
Nunes, Rafael Aboase, De Casseres, Jacob Nassy, etc.
The quotation to go with the map was suggested by
Rabbi J. Van Gelder of Utrecht, and was probably
prompted by the position of the community that was
separated by the river.

109

THE SAMSON FOUNTAIN

Czechoslovakia: 1940
(Bohemia and Moravia—
during German Occupation)
Samson Fountain

. . . and, behold, a young lion
roared against him. And the spirit
of the Lord came mightily upon
him, and he rent him as one
would have rent a kid, . . .

Judges 14:5-6

IN the Czech city of Budweis stands the Samson Fountain, erected in the year 1720. It depicts the figure of
Samson, astride a lion and tearing its jaws open. Samson's strength gave rise to many legends. One of these
tales is that Samson uprooted two mountains and rubbed
them against one another till they turned to dust. That
Samson's likeness should be fashioned into a decorative
fountain commanding a city plaza was not considered
unusual in God-fearing Czechoslovakia of the eighteenth
century. But that this biblical Jewish hero should be
commemorated on a stamp issued by a regime dedicated
to extermination of Jews is a strange fact. The German
Nazi government of Bohemia and Moravia (Czechoslovakia in 1940 under German rule) could hardly have
been ignorant of the meaning of the story of Samson.

110

SAMSON THE STRONG MAN

And Samson went and caught three hundred foxes, and took torches, and turned tail to tail, and put a torch in the midst between every two tails. And when he had set the torches on fire, he let them go into the standing corn of the Philistines, . . .

Judges 15:4-5

Israel: 1961
Warriors of Israel

DESPITE his tremendous strength, Samson did not rally the Hebrews into a fighting group against the Philistines—their chief enemy in his day. The Philistines were well organized into a league of city states and they dominated the southern part of Canaan. No state of war really existed between the Hebrews and the Philistines. Samson's actions therefore were related to private quarrels and motivated by a wish for personal revenge.

Popular belief usually names Delilah as Samson's mate. However, he was married to another Philistine, a Timnite woman who also betrayed him by revealing the answer to his riddle to her male friends. He burned the Philistine fields out of anger at her family for yet another betrayal. Interestingly, the Timnite wife is not once mentioned by name in the Bible. Delilah, who was a harlot, came into his life after the death of his wife and her father by burning, a punishment meted out by the Philistines in reaction to Samson's deed.

SAMSON AND DELILAH

Hungary: 1970
"Samson and Delilah"
by Michel Rocca

And she made him sleep upon her knees; and she called for a man, and had the seven locks of his head shaven off; and she began to afflict him, and his strength went from him.

Judges 16:19

SAMSON's superhuman strength was proven time and again. As though the biblical narrative were not enough, folklore added even further to the unbelievable tales about Samson. The Bible tells how he tore a lion in two, when it attacked him; how he easily tore loose from new ropes that held him captive and killed a thousand men, with "a jaw bone of an ass" as his only weapon, when they surrounded him. Folklore goes further, claiming that he uprooted mature trees and even mountains with his bare hands. His strength was in his hair, particularly in seven golden strands of hair. Legend holds that whenever Samson was engaged in a feat of superhuman strength, his hair would vibrate, making a bell-like sound which could be heard many miles away.

SAMSON AND THE PHILISTINES

Spain: 1966
"Audacity" by Jose Sert

And Samson said: 'Let me die with the Philistines.' And he bent with all his might; and the house fell upon the lords, and upon all the people that were therein. So the dead that he slew at his death were more than they that he slew in his life.

Judges: 16:30

SAMSON was a Nazirite: one who was consecrated and thereby set apart. The name was applied to a group of persons who took a special vow to God that they would not partake in any form of fruit of the vine; that they would abstain from cutting their hair; would avoid contact with the dead; and that they would refrain from eating all unclean food.

There are inconsistencies in the Samson story when seen in this light. He pays his wager when his riddle is solved by slaying thirty men and giving their garments to those he was obliged to reward. This seems to involve at least contact with the dead. However, Samson was unselfish and generally of service to his people with no thought of reward. His obvious weakness was his fondness for beautiful women. The folk legends forgive him all his faults. He is described as a shield to his people even after his death. For twenty years after Samson had died, the Philistines did not attack the Israelites out of their fear of him.

AN ANCIENT
HEBREW COIN

*. . . for a piece of silver and a loaf
of bread . . .*

I Samuel 2:36

Israel: 1960

AN ancient Hebrew coin from the time of the War of
the Second Temple is shown on this stamp. The stamp
motif is the same as that on the very first Israeli stamps
which all depicted similar coins. The theme of ancient
coins was especially chosen to symbolize the connection
between the ancient Jewish state and the new modern-day
State of Israel. The coins date from the two Jewish wars
of liberation against the Roman Empire, in 67–70 C.E.
and 132–135 C.E. On this stamp, as on the others, the
lettering on the coin is in the ancient Hebrew script,
which, at the time the coins were struck, had already
long been replaced by the square lettering used to this
day.

THE INFANT SAMUEL

And it came to pass at that time, when Eli was laid down in his place—now his eyes had begun to wax dim, that he could not see—and the lamp of God was not yet gone out, and Samuel was laid down to sleep in the temple of the Lord, where the ark of God was, that the Lord called Samuel; and he said: 'Here am I.'

I Samuel 3:2-4

Australia: 1957
Christmas Stamp
The Prophet Samuel
as a Child

To mark the holiday season of Christmas, Australia issued a stamp set showing a young child kneeling in prayer before what appears to be a cross of light. After much debate, with reports attributing the design to a variety of possibilities, it was determined that it came from a painting by Sir Joshua Reynolds showing the prophet Samuel as a child and titled *The Infant Samuel*. The original painting by Reynolds was destroyed in 1816 in a fire at Belvoir Castle. Two known repetitions exist, however; one at the Tate Gallery in London and the other in Montpelier, France in the Musée Fabre. At the close of his career in painting, Reynolds became interested in painting children in different mythological and historical connections. This is one of them. The design shows Samuel as the Bible describes, him, a very young child already showing the mark of prophesy.

115

SAUL—FIRST KING OF ISRAEL

Now there was a man of Benjamin, whose name was Kish, the son of Abiel, . . . And he had a son, whose name was Saul, young and goodly, and there was not among the children of Israel a goodlier person than he: from his shoulders and upward he was higher than any of the people.

I Samuel 9:1-2

Israel: 1960
Rosh Hashana 5721
King Saul

THE better to understand the confusing narration of Saul attaining the role of king, one authority suggests that the biblical description be separated into its three component parts. One strand presents the prophet Samuel disagreeing with the people about the merits of having a king at all (1 Samuel 8.10–18), but finally accepting their position and choosing Saul, by lot, to be king at Mizpah (1 Samuel 10: 17–27). Another strand presents Samuel as very pleased to have found the right man and secretly anointing him (1 Samuel 9:1 to 1 Samuel 10–16). In the third section Saul, angered by the plight of the men of Jabesh at the hands of the Ammonites, assumes the role of gathering the separated Israelites together and defeats the Ammonites; whereupon he is anointed king at Gilgal (1 Samuel 11).

Mohammedan folklore has an altogether different version of who became the first king of Israel. Their view is that it was not a Benjamite named Saul but an Egyptian named Taluth. In their version, too, Samuel chooses him and anoints him and opposition is silenced when the anointed bravely leads the people in victorious battle against an oppressor.

116

DAVID—GREATEST KING
OF ISRAEL

And it came to pass, when the (evil) spirit from God was upon Saul, that David took the harp, and played with his hand; so Saul found relief, and it was well with him, and the evil spirit departed from him.

I Samuel 16:23

Israel: 1960
Kings of Israel
New Year Holiday

D AVID is regarded as the greatest of the kings of Israel. The facets of his personality are many—any one of his talents being remarkably developed and enough to mark his name in history. Although he was a shepherd until he attained manhood, he demonstrated genius in government administration and organization, unifying the nation and centralizing authority. He divided the country into districts (to permit a better administrative system, making it easier to collect taxes as well as to break the hold of tribal thinking). He also reorganized and improved the army. As a result, he enlarged the kingdom as well. Yet he was well loved by his people, both in his day and later. In part, it was his role in securing the City of David (now Jerusalem) and making it both the political and military capital as well as the religious center that endeared him to the people. He was seen as especially chosen by God, and as such his religious zeal was inspirational. So, too, was his musicianship in composing as well as in skillfully playing. He was further admired as a hero-warrior. All this in a lifetime of seventy years of fascinating interpersonal complexities.

In light of the above, the folklore account that David was predestined to death within hours of his birth is especially intriguing. The legend accounts for David's life as a gift from Adam, who foresaw David's untimely death and gave up seventy years from his own allotted thousand.

DAVID AND GOLIATH

And David ran, and stood over the Philistine, and took his sword, and drew it out of the sheath thereof, and slew him, and cut off his head therewith.

I Samuel 17:51

Malta: 1965
Commemorating the Great
Siege of 1565

IN the year 1565, the island of Malta was attacked by Suleiman the Magnificent. That event is still known in Christian history as the Great Seige. The forces of Suleiman expected to overwhelm the poorly equipped garrison easily and move on to a conquest of southern Europe. The seige lasted for four months and was finally lifted because the attacking armada was decimated.

Four hundred years later, Malta issued this stamp commemorating the Great Seige. The stamp shows the two faces of the victory medal celebrating the event. The biblical scene of David severing the head of Goliath appears on one face of the medal, as a symbol of how the tiny Malta garrison fought off a well-equipped Turkish armada more than four times its size.

DAVID
THE HERO

Liberia: 1969
Famous Paintings Set
"David and Goliath" by
Caravaggio

*And David took
the head of the
Philistine, and
brought it to
Jerusalem; but he
put his armour in
his tent.*

I Samuel 17:54

IT is a little-known fact that it is not at all certain that the giant Goliath was slain by David. The man who slew Goliath in 2 Samuel 21:19 is called Elhanan the son of Jaare-oregim. Another version of the same account later in 1 Chronicles 20:5 explains that the giant slain by Elhanan the son of Jaare-oregim was not Goliath but Lachmi, the brother of Goliath the Hittite.

Nor is Goliath the only giant to oppose and to be slain by Israelite warriors. In addition to Goliath slain by David and Lachmi slain by Elhanan, there was Ishbi-benob who at the point of subduing David was felled by Abishai; then Saph who was also described as "of the sons of the giant" and who was killed by Sibbecai the Hushathite; and an unnamed especially fearsome giant with six fingers on each hand and six toes on each foot who was brought down by Jonathan son of Shimea.

AN ANCIENT MUSICAL INSTRUMENT

Israel: 1956
Festival Stamps

And David and all the house of Israel played . . . with timbrels and with sistra, . . .

II Samuel 6:5

IT is impossible to know the character of early Hebrew music with certainty. The liturgy of the synagogue has been transformed by the music of the peoples amongst whom the Jews lived. The instruments, however, can be reconstructed with greater accuracy. Monuments, tombs, and other documentation of ancient peoples depict either the same musical instruments or kindred ones. The timbrel was probably much like today's tambourine, a small hand drum which could not be tightened or loosened to regulate the pitch. Sistra (an artist's conception is shown on the stamp) were of the percussion type and were fashioned with loose metallic rings on rods. The Egyptian goddess Isis is typically described or depicted in paintings and statues as holding a sistrum in her right hand. According to Plutarch, the purpose of her sistrum was to remind people that everything must be kept in continual agitation; so that when corruption clogs the nature of things, motion shakes out the problem.

KING DAVID DISPENSES JUSTICE

Israel: 1969
"King David" by Marc Chagall

*And David reigned over all
Israel; and David executed justice
and righteousness unto all his
people.*

II Samuel 8:15

T HE painting of King David by Marc Chagall is one of a series of biblical pictures by the artist painted between 1950 and 1956. Chagall's style is known as "psychic reality"; it is part early Surrealist, part Expressionist, and entirely symbolic and poetic. He blends together Jewish motifs and symbols in a colorful expression of realism and fantasy that delve into the unconscious and present memories mixed with dreams.

The son of a grocery clerk and a mother who had no formal education, Chagall was born in Vitebsk, Russia, in 1887. He was the only son among eight sisters in a family that not only read the Bible but lived it. From his Hassidic uncle Noah, who played the violin for Marc by the hour and, by the hour, told him sacred stories, he learned a feeling of ecstatic communication as well as escape into a world of Scriptures and dreams.

The negotiations for reproducing the King David painting on a stamp took about two years. At stake was the problem of how to execute the intricate and colorful design so as to do justice to the artist's work, and yet to be within the limits of stamp reproduction.

BATH-SHEBA
AT HER BATH

And it came to pass at eventide,
that David arose from off his bed,
and walked upon the roof
of the king's house; and from the roof
he saw a woman bathing; and the woman
was very beautiful to look upon.

Hungary: 1968
"Bath-sheba at Her Ba
by Sebastiano Ricci

II Samuel 11:2

To publicize the art treasures and exhibits in the Budapest Museum of Fine Arts, Hungary issued this stamp on a miniature sheet. The painting by Sebastiano Ricci of *Bath-sheba at Her Bath* shows a small David in the top left background watching the proceedings. The Bible details how David fell in love with Bath-sheba and had her husband Uriah return with a letter to his commander requiring Uriah to be placed in the thick of battle so that he would be killed. The Uriah letter is a Hebrew version of a widespread folktale with parallels in Greek lore, in Hindu and Arabic tales, and even in Shakespeare (*Hamlet*). None, however, convey the biblical moral lesson of the prophet Nathan. He confronts the king and tells the tale of the rich man who takes away his poor neighbor's only ewe. Nathan identifies the culprit as the king himself when David demands to know the name of so evil a person. "You are that man" says Nathan, blaming David for stealing Uriah's Bath-sheba.

BATH-SHEBA
THE WIFE OF URIAH

Ajman: 1970
"Bath-sheba"
by Rembrandt

*And David sent and inquired
after the woman. And one
said: 'Is not this Bath-sheba,
the daughter of Eliam, the
wife of Uriah the Hittite?'*

II Samuel 11:3

DAVID the king is one of the most beloved personalities of Jewish history. It is believed that the Messiah will come from the House of David. It is remarkable, then, that the biblical story recounting David's lust for Bath-sheba was not edited out by the authors (divine or otherwise) responsible for the Bible. David committed murder to satisfy his desire for Bath-sheba. This certainly cannot be deemed a model of behavior for later generations to follow, but there is a lesson here. Even the greatest is presented in the fullness of both good and evil. David, who loves God and is the sweet singer of psalms to God, also has his dark side. As do we all! David will be held accountable for his sin, but there is the reminder in this episode that we all have a sinister nature within us. Even when we give in to our evil impulses, however, we still have not sunk forever. The task remains, to keep striving towards God.

Rembrandt was especially intrigued by the human nature of Bible personalities, more than by cosmic happenings. Perhaps his interest stemmed from his physical proximity to the People of the Book. He lived in the Jewish quarter in Amsterdam later in life, and many of his models for biblical characters came from the ghetto and have Semitic features.

SOLOMON—KING OF ISRAEL

Israel: 1960
Kings of Israel
New Year 5721

*Give therefore Thy servant an
understanding heart to judge
Thy people, that I may discern
between good and evil; for who
is able to judge this Thy great
people?*
                    I Kings 3:9

IT was the intention of the artist, Asher Kalderon, in designing a set of stamps picturing the first three kings of Israel, to emphasize a major characteristic of each. All three are shown in the pattern of stained-glass windows. Saul projects militancy, while David depicts spirituality, and Solomon (shown on this stamp) conveys wisdom and righteousness.

To this end, the artist shows Solomon holding a set of scales in one hand and a scroll with a design of the Temple in the other. While it is clear that only the truly wise can mete out justice, only the truly righteous would be permitted to build God's Temple, which was the main project of Solomon's life.

Despite the choice of Solomon to build the Temple, he is also seen as having so transgressed in his lifetime that the Temple was later destroyed. A folk tale tells that Solomon, having fallen in love with an Egyptian princess, offered her as a wedding gift the toll to be levied on all who entered the gates to the city of Jerusalem. At the moment of Solomon's offer, the angel Gabriel planted a reed in the sea. About this reed sediment accumulated which ultimately became an island. Upon this land arose the city of Rome whence came the destruction of Solomon's Temple.

SOLOMON THE JUDGE

Liberia: 1969
Famous Paintings Set
"The Judgement of Solomon"
by Giorgione

*And the king said: 'Fetch me a
sword'. And they brought a
sword before the king.' And the
king said: 'Divide the living child
in two, and give half to the one,
and half to the other.'*

I Kings 3:24-25

THIS well-known Bible story has many parallels in
world folklore. Some of the more interesting ones differ
in that they describe an alternate means of determining
the true parent. A Buddhist tale describes how one child
was stolen by a female cannibal demon (yakinni) who
then claimed the child, as did the mother. Buddha suggests a tug of war, with the child as the object being
tugged—which, of course, the true mother refuses. Another instance that comes from China has the child
thrown into the water with a live fish in its clothing. As
the fish struggles to get free, the true mother sees her
child being harmed and dives in to the rescue.

In another example which comes from Cairo, two men
claim fatherhood of the same child. The judge decrees
that the child be starved for three days and then fed a
bowl of milk. Given the milk, the hungry child greedily
gulps and spills it. It is the true father who excuses this
behavior while the other scolds the child for its bad man-
ners.

KING SOLOMON
AND THE QUEEN
OF SHEBA

Yemen: 1968
Queen of Sheba's Visit to
King Solomon

Then spoke the woman
whose the living child was
unto the king, for her heart
yearned upon her son, and
she said: 'Oh, my Lord, give
her the living child, and in
no wise slay it.' But the other
said: 'It shall be neither mine
nor thine; divide it.'

I Kings 3:26

In discussing myths and folk tales, the folklorist Stith Thomson concludes that we cannot be certain about the origins of myths. Possibly there was a myth-making period in man's history; but probably, whenever conditions are right there are forces that make for the production of myths. Despite the variety of cultural patterns throughout the world and down through the ages, people all have the same human needs, and hence there will be similar acts and thoughts. It becomes, therefore, unlikely that one can accurately trace the actual origin of a given folk tale or myth.

For all of this, some authorities point to India as the location of the beginnings of this story. Their argument is built on the practical matter that in India a childless widow has no right to inheritance, so that it would be more probable that two women claiming the same man's estate should both make claim on the child.

THE CEDARS OF
THE LEBANON

Lebanon: 1937

*Now therefore command thou
that they hew me cedar-trees out
of Lebanon; . . . and I will give
thee hire for thy servants according
to all that thou shalt say; for thou
knowest that there is not among
us any that hath skill to hew
timber like unto the Zidonians.*

I Kings 5:20

T HE cedar of Lebanon is a magnificent tree growing
to nearly a hundred feet with outstretched horizontal
limbs that give welcome shade. It has an extremely dur-
able wood, rich in resin, which both resists worms and
lends itself to taking a high polish. As a result, it is a
valuable timber for building. It also carves well. Not
surprisingly, therefore, it was chosen by Solomon for use
in the Temple.

The association of cedar trees with biblical life is not
restricted to construction of the House of God. It was
customary to plant a tree in the garden to mark the birth
of a new-born child. A cedar was planted for a son and
a pine for a daughter. Wood from these self-same cedars
and pines was later used to build a bridal chamber for a
betrothed couple. A folk belief maintained a mysterious
relationship between the life of a person and the growth
of a tree.

129

SOLOMON'S WALL

Yemen: 1968
Queen of Sheba's Visit to
King Solomon

*For the house, when it was
in building, was built of
stone made ready at the
quarry; and there was
neither hammer nor axe nor
any tool of iron heard in the
house, while it was in
building.*

I Kings 6:7

T HIS stamp from Yemen identifies the wall shown on it as "Solomon's Wall." In truth, while it is all that today remains of the Temple it is most likely a remnant of Herod's work rather than the work of Solomon. Solomon's Temple was destroyed in 586 B.C.E. It was rebuilt a second time sixty years later, and was called the Temple of the Maccabees, as it was rededicated by Judah Maccabee in 164 BCE. King Herod, a master builder, rebuilt the Temple in 20 B.C.E. even though the Second Temple was still standing at that time. Nor is it likely that these three temples were the only ones in Jerusalem on this location. Prior to Solomon's Temple, the Holy Ark with the original Ten Commandments was brought by David to Jerusalem. It is certain that some sort of structure housed the Ark, probably on the same site, until the Temple was built.

However, for Yemen, an Arab state technically at war with Israel at the time, to show the Temple Wall on a stamp, is an action difficult to comprehend. It could only serve as an additional reminder of Israel's victory in the 1967 Six-Day War. In fact, Israel showed the same wall on its stamps only a year previously as a way of marking its victory in that battle, and to mark, also, the unification of Jerusalem.

THE WESTERN WALL

Israel: 1967
Western Wall of the Temple
Victory in the Six-Day War

And the Lord said unto him:
'I have heard thy prayer and
thy supplication, that thou
hast made before Me: I have
hallowed this house, which
thou hast built, to put My
name there for ever; and
Mine eyes and My heart
shall be there perpetually.

I Kings 9:3

DENIED access to the only known remnant of the Holy
Temple for the two decades that saw Jerusalem a divided
city, the Israelis were exultant to have won back their
"Wailing Wall." The wall was never part of the building
that was the Temple itself. It is rather a retaining wall
and marks the western border of the Temple Mount.
Jews have called it the Western Wall, but the sight of annual ceremonies when observant Orthodox Jews prayed
and wept recalling the destruction of the Temple, led to
the name "Wailing Wall."

A careful examination of the bottom row on the Israeli stamp shows how each stone has a hewn border
around its perimeter. This is an index of Herod's building. On the wall itself, the four or so courses of stone
immediately above the ground are of this type. (So, too,
are the extensive number of rows that are buried deep

132

underneath the ground and support the whole structure.) The next many layers on top of the Herodian blocks are smaller and obviously were put in place much later. Most interesting is the third section at the top consisting of the smallest stones of all. (For a better view, see the Yemenite stamp identifying the wall as Solomon's wall.) Insofar as the wall is a retaining wall, it is so built that the level of ground on one side is much higher than on the other. This permitted objects and refuse to be hurled over the wall at the praying Jews on the other side below. To end this, the British philanthropist Moses Montefiore had the wall raised by adding the layers of stone at the top.

KING SOLOMON'S NAVY

Israel: 1957
Honoring of the Merchant Marine

*And King Solomon made a
navy of ships in Ezion-geber
which is beside Elath, on the
shore of the Red Sea, in the
land of Edom.*

I Kings 9:26

THE boundaries of Solomon's kingdom represent the climax of power of the early Hebrew nation, and the fulfillment of the promise of Canaan.

By cementing an alliance with Hiram of Tyre, Solomon obtained the skills in shipbuilding and navigation that permitted an extensive trade through the Red Sea to Africa and even to India.

This involved holding under his control the area of Edom where Elath gave entry to the Gulf of Aqaba. Not only did Solomon hold this land, he also made use of its riches. Archeological evidence uncovered by Nelson Glueck in the 1930s confirms that Solomon mined the minerals in the land of Edom, even building an extensive metal manufacturing city on the Gulf of Aqaba (Ezion-geber).

The Edomites, according to some researchers, were probably descended from Esau. If so, the Israelites and Edomites were kin, tracing their antecedents to their mutual father, Isaac, and their enmity to the episode of Esau's being tricked out of his birthright by Jacob.

SOLOMON'S FAME
SPREADS AFAR

*And when the Queen of Sheba
heard of the fame of Solomon
because of the name of the Lord,
she came to prove him with hard
questions.*

I Kings 10:1

Ethiopia: 1964
The Queen of Sheba

E VIDENCE points to an actual place, called Sheba in the Bible, located in southwestern Arabia in the vicinity of present-day Yemen. However, it is much more difficult to be definite about the queen who was supposed to have visited Jerusalem. The Bible is the only record of such a personage and of such a visit. Nor does the Bible give the queen a name. In later days, an Arab myth gives her the name Balkis, which is the name she is, therefore, assigned in the Koran.

The Ethiopians hold to the tradition that Queen Balkis is of their nation. There is that possibility. Modern Ethiopia is removed from Yemen or ancient Sheba by a mere twenty miles of the Red Sea at that point. Contact between the two and even domination of one over the other probably occurred.

In light of the lack of a biblical name for the Queen of Sheba, it is interesting that on this Ethiopian stamp (from a set of Ethiopian queens) she is identified, not as Balkis, but as "Sheba 990 B.C." In fact the evidence from early history of that region indicates it was ruled by men who carried a title equivalent to "priest-king."

135

THE CARAVAN OF SHEBA

Yemen: 1968
Queen of Sheba's Visit to King Solomon

*And she came to Jerusalem
with a very great train,
with camels that bore spices
and gold very much,
and precious stones; . . .*

I Kings 10:2

J EWISH folk tales embellish the romantic notion of the visit of a glamorous queen to pay homage to the wisest of all kings. Among other fanciful details, one narrates how she filled her ships with silver and gold as well as precious stones and rare woods along with many treasures. As though this were not gift enough, she also sent six thousand boys and girls who were of identical age and chosen for their grace and beauty. These gifts preceded her by three years. On her arrival, she was greeted by Solomon's servant Benaiah, who impressed her so much she thought he was Solomon. Learning Benaiah was only the servant made her feel awe at the thought of meeting the master.

SOLOMON THE WISE

Yemen: 1968
Queen of Sheba's Visit
to King Solomon

*And Solomon told her all her
questions; there was not any thing
hid from the king which he told
her not.*

I Kings 10:3

T HERE is a definite sectarian emphasis in the Jewish folktale in which the Queen of Sheba asks questions of King Solomon. While some have a universal meaning, most are taken from the biblical history of the Jewish patriarchs. Some examples follow:

"Question: 'What is the land upon which the sun shown only once?' Answer: 'It is the land of the sea when the waters were divided for one day by Moses.'

"Question: 'Three ate and drank on earth yet were not born of male and female. Who are they?' Answer: 'The three angels who visited Abraham.'

"Question: 'A woman said to her son, "Your father is my father and your grandfather is my husband, you are my son and I am your sister." Who was she? Answer: 'Lot's daughter talking to her son.' "

THE QUEEN
OF SHEBA

Yemen: 1968
Queen of Sheba's Visit
to Solomon

*". . . Howbeit I believed not the
words, until I came, and mine
eyes had seen it; and behold, the
half was not told me; thou hast
wisdom and prosperity exceeding
the fame which I heard. . . ."*

I Kings 10:7

THE story of the Queen of Sheba's visit to Solomon is
also found in the Moslem Koran. An interesting detail
in that telling is that Solomon had an overlay of glass
placed on the floor of his court of audience. This was
mistakenly perceived by the Queen of Sheba as a pool of
water, and she is described as lifting her skirts to wade
through it. Later retellings of the episode explain that
somehow Solomon had heard rumors that the Queen of
Sheba had unusually ugly legs, and this was his way of
seeing for himself. The tales further add that her legs
were not deformed in any way, but were in fact attractive.
Solomon is portrayed as having been so taken by his
vision of her charms that he added her to his harem.

138

And King Solomon
gave to the Queen of Sheba
all her desire, whatever she asked,
beside that which Solomon
gave her of his royal bounty. . . .

Yemen: 1968
Queen of Sheba's Vis
to King Solomon

I Kings 10:13

T HE arrangement of a pair of stamps of different values or design that are joined together, such as the stamps shown here picturing the visit to King Solomon by the Queen, is known as *"se tenant"* to stamp collectors from the French meaning "joined together." Sometimes a pair of stamps are placed together with one right side up, and the other upside down. Such a pair is called *"tête-bêche."*

Another common pairing infrequently seen by the non-collector is one where some blank space is left between the stamps—although the space may sometimes be decorated with a design. These are gutter pairs which may be found with *se tenant* or *tête-bêche printings.* There is usually some appropriate reason for these unusual printing arrangements, such as later convenient assembling into booklets for sale to the stamp-using public wanting a given small quantity of stamps in a convenient package.

THE DEPARTURE
OF THE QUEEN
OF SHEBA

Yemen: 1968
Queen of Sheba's Visit
to Solomon

*. . . So she turned and went
to her own land, she and her
servants.*

I Kings 10:13

ACCORDING to Ethiopian belief, there was indeed a romance between King Solomon and the Queen of Sheba. In some Ethiopian writings the Queen of Sheba is known by the name Makeda. A new dynasty in the thirteenth century justified itself as being of royal birth claiming its descent from Menelik, who was represented as being the son of King Solomon born to the Queen of Sheba.

In recognition of the Solomonic lineage, the Ethiopian Emperor who is still today a direct descendant of Menelik I, is known as the Conquering Lion of the Tribe of Judah. His royal throne is known as Solomon's Throne.

KING SOLOMON'S THRONE

*Moreover the king made a great
throne of ivory, and overlaid it
with the finest gold. There were
six steps to the throne, and the
top of the throne was round
behind; and there were arms on
either side by the place of the seat,
and two lions standing beside the
arms. And twelve lions stood
there on the one side and on the
other upon the six steps; there
was not the like made in any
kingdom.*

Abyssinia: 1909
King Solomon's Throne

I Kings 10:18-20

D ESPITE the description of Solomon's throne in the
Bible, the popular tales made it even more magnificent
in their telling. Not only was it made of ivory overlaid
with gold, but in the folk tales it was decorated with
rubies, emeralds, and other precious stones. Golden eagles
were added to the lions flanking the throne. On each
step an unlikely pair of animals wrought of pure gold
faced one another—symbols that the weak need not fear
the strong in the search for justice. On the first step an
ox faced a lion; on the second step were a lamb and
wolf; on the third were a goat and leopard; on the fourth
were an eagle and peacock; etc. Hanging above the throne
was a candelabrum bearing the names and images of
great personages of the past up to that time.

141

ELIJAH THE FUGITIVE

Columbia: 1968
"Elijah Hiding in the
Wilderness" by Vasquez
Thirty-Fourth Eucharistic
Congress

*And he lay down and slept under
a broomtree; and, behold, an
angel touched him, and said unto
him: 'Arise and eat.' And he
looked, and behold, there was at
his head a cake baked on the hot
stones, and a cruse of water.*

I Kings 19:5-6

E UCHARIST is the earliest title for the sacrament of
the body and blood of Christ. It is based on the giving
of thanks or *eucharistia* with which Jesus set apart his
bread and wine at the Last Supper as memorials of himself. This of course was a deviation from the usual ritual
of the Passover celebration, which the Last Supper was.
Typically the Passover celebration follows a prescribed
order of rituals, so that, in fact, the celebration is called
Seder meaning "order."

The broom tree is common in the Palestine-Sinai
desert, and in many places it is the only shade; it sometimes grows to a height of seven to ten feet. Its roots are
still used today to make charcoal. It's scientific name is
fetama retem.

ELIJAH ASCENDS INTO HEAVEN

Vatican: 1938
Ascent of Elijah to Heaven

*And it came to pass, as they still
went on, and talked, that, behold
there appeared a chariot of fire,
and horses of fire, which parted
them both asunder and Elijah
went up by a whirlwind into
heaven.*

II Kings 2:11

THE ascension to heaven is not exclusively a Bible tract. It appears in various forms in ancient literatures of other peoples as, for example, in the Greek mythology of Apollo who traverses the heavens in his chariot in his role of sun god. In most accounts of such ascensions, there are characteristic details. Usually the event occurs beside a body of water; it often involves a chariot or wagon; there is, typically, fire enveloping the action leaving a trail of sparks; and it is associated with a storm, or a sudden blast of wind.

The ascension of Elijah in a fiery chariot driven by fiery horses is a dramatic yet most appropriate ending for so impressive and awesome a man. His courageous, dedicated opposition to the idol-worship cult of the reigning royal couple, and his vigorous championing of justice leads to the belief that he deserves not to die, but to be transferred living from earth to heaven. Given the belief

143

that Elijah was transported alive to heaven, it becomes understandable that he may return alive to earth later.

In the folk mind Elijah became so important a personage that his memory remained constant in the ensuing generations. Wonders and miracles were attributed to him and, ultimately, some began to assign to him a heavenly identity. Some even believed him to be an angel who had won permission from God to spend time on earth being helpful to deserving individuals in need.

THE PROPHET ISAIAH

Vatican: 1964
Celebration of Michelangelo's
400th Anniversary
"Isaiah" by Michelangelo

*The vision of Isaiah the son of
Amoz, which he saw concerning
Judah and Jerusalem, in the days
of Uzziah, Jotham, Ahaz, and
Hezekiah, kings of Judah.*

Isaiah 1:1

THE critical dates in the assumption of the throne, among the kings listed in Isaiah, are established. It is possible, therefore, to determine when Isaiah undertook his prophetic role. Uzziah became king in the year 780 B.C.E. and Hezekiah died in the year 692 B.C.E.

The major emphasis in Isaiah's teaching is on the need for Judah to look to God for guidance not only in how each individual conducts his own life, but also in relation to the political decisions the country should make. Any rituals, religious or otherwise, that are devoid of trust in God are empty. Any political alliances that are not built out of faith in God are doomed, and probably destructive. God is Israel's king and because Israel will not place their trust and faith in Him, they will be destroyed, except for a remnant that will survive.

PEACE ON EARTH

Hungary: 1962
United Nations: 1967
Call for Suspension of
Nuclear Testing

They shall beat their swords into plowshares, . . .

Isaiah 2:4

THESE familiar closing lines from Isaiah's vision of peace are inscribed on the wall of the United Nations Plaza. However, they were also evoked in connection with the United Nations General Assembly call to all nations to suspend nuclear weapons testing. It is as a part of that UN declaration that these stamps in six languages were printed.

Previously the idea embodied in the words was captured in a design of the Soviet Union and later in a similar design used by Hungary.

THE SETTLEMENT
OF ISRAEL

Israel: 1952
70th Anniversary of "Bilu"

O house of Jacob, come, let us
go up. . . .

Isaiah 2:5

As prophesied by Isaiah, the Israelites and then the Judeans were conquered and exiled. Unlike other nations who had suffered the same fate, the Hebrews held tenaciously to their identity as well as their religion. The wish to return to the land of their fathers is as old as the Babylonian exile which dates back to 586 B.C.E.

In the past century various attempts to build a Jewish homeland took form. Among the Zionists, as these groups came to be called, was an occasional group of Jews that undertook colonization projects in Palestine. One particular group of lovers of Zion who were the first East European Jews to establish an agricultural colony in the Holy Land called itself "BILU." Its name came from the acronym (a word formed by taking the first letter of each word in a phrase, etc.) of Isaiah 2:5. "O house of Jacob, come ye and let us walk in the light of the Lord." In the Hebrew "Beth Yaakov, Lechu U'nalchah" permits the acronym to develop as BILU. Israel issued this stamp to commemorate the seventieth anniversary of the Bilu that built such settlements as Rosh Pinah, Rishon-Le-Zion, Zichron Yaakov, and Gederah.

147

ISAIAH, THE FORETELLER OF THE MESSIAH

*Therefore the Lord Himself shall
give you a sign: behold, the
young woman shall conceive,
and bear a son, and shall call his
name Immanuel.*
Isaiah 7:14

Italy: 1961
"Isaiah"
by Michelangelo

O N the significance of this comment by Isaiah there
has been and probably will continue to be much controversy. Many Christian scholars and theologians read this
to be a prediction of the Virgin birth. Hebrew scholars
(and also some Christian scholars today) point out that
the translation in the King James version of the Bible
text as "virgin" instead of "young woman" is inaccurate.

Isaiah was challenging the Judean King Ahaz to "ask
a sign of God," thereby obtaining the means to convince
Ahaz that Isaiah spoke for God in urging Ahaz to make
no move to get help from Assyria in the face of Judea being attacked by Syria and Israel. When Ahaz would not
ask for a sign from God, Isaiah angrily offered one any-
way with the statement "the young woman shall conceive . . ." Ahaz was not convinced.

The name Immanuel translated from the Hebrew reads
"God is with us," which further encouraged those who
saw in this prediction the birth of Jesus.

There is a group of myths, predating this period, that
tell of the birth of a "Wondrous Child" as a beginning of
the coming of an "Age of Bliss." Usually the birth of the
Wondrous Child follows a sacred marriage between a
god and consort, usually a goddess. Some pagan groups
actually developed a ceremony to celebrate and sometimes duplicate the nuptials. Brick couches used in such
ceremonies have been unearthed in ancient civilizations.

PEACE ON EARTH

Israel: 1962
Rosh Hashana
5723

*And the wolf shall dwell with the
lamb, . . .
And the leopard shall lie down
with the kid; . . .*

Isaiah 11:6

BECAUSE the Bible has stimulated men not only by virtue of its spiritual content, it has been analyzed to discover the sources of the magnificent literary power it conveys. In large measure the Bible is characterized by dynamic terse writing which is vivid and uses memorable phrasing. "Picture language" is utilized in place of abstractions. Whether the particular section is narrative, poetry, drama, wisdom literature or prophesy, the phraseology is striking.

Hebrew poetry often sets up a special relationship between the lines so that in a given two-line couplet an idea is first stated, and then reinforced by being restated in a different but related way. Occasionally the impact is reinforced by a parallelism having a contrasting rather than a synonymous thought.

In this philatelic statement of a couplet from Isaiah's vision of the ideal world, we see an example of synonymous parallelism as well as "picture language."

149

THE IDEAL KINGDOM

Israel: 1962
Rosh Hashana 5723

*And the suckling child shall
    play on the hole of the asp,
And the weaned child shall
    put his hand on the
    basilisk's den.*

Isaiah 11:8

CLEARLY the ideal kingdom envisaged by Isaiah is one where all of creation is restored to the peace of the garden of Eden. All creatures live side by side without fear and in tranquility. To express this thought in its extremest form, the picture of an innocent infant playing with venomous snakes is painted for the listener.

There is much controversy as to what kind of serpent is described in the second half of the couplet. Some translations read "basilisk," others read "adder." At one time the word was usually rendered as "cockatrice," which is probably a mythical serpent with a cock's comb or crown whose very breath could cause death, and who could kill merely by a look.

Serpents identified as being found in that part of the world number more than thirty different species.

A SEASON FOR
GLADNESS

Ye shall have a song
As in the night when a
feast is hallowed;
And gladness of heart, as
when one goeth with the
pipe
To come unto the mountains
of the Lord, to the Rock of
Israel.

Israel: 1956

Isaiah 30:29

ANNUALLY, on the occasion of the Jewish New Year, Israel issues commemorative stamps to honor the event. Invariably the stamps carry holiday greetings in Hebrew, "moadim v'simcha." This stems from the greeting of the Jerusalem pilgrims: ". . . and with love hast thou given us, O Lord, our God, solemn days for joy, festivals and seasons for gladness." The Sephardim (Spanish and Portuguese Jews and their descendants) may be credited with the preservation of this salutation which has been used in this manner: The greeter says, "Solemn days for joy," and the greeted replies with the conclusion of the prayer, "festivals and seasons for gladness."

MAKING THE DESERT
A GARDEN

*And the desert shall rejoice and
blossom as the rose.*

Isaiah 35:1

Israel: 1953
Conquest of the Desert

T HE agricultural potential of Israel is quite limited by
virtue of both climate and geography. Rainfall, while ade-
quate, is restricted to a seasonal downpour. Much of the
area is desert, and large segments have been robbed of
their fecundity through misuse. The Ottoman Empire
denuded the land by stripping most of the timber-produc-
ing trees for lumber. The goats raised by the Bedouin
further depleted the growth of soil-retaining and soil-en-
riching plant life.

Israel, therefore, has put intensive efforts into exploring
all kinds of ways to make the land productive. Of particular interest is the desert which, because of its size,
encourages experimentation. Historical antecedents of
deserts that were made to bloom can be found in the
ancient Nabataean civilization which expertly utilized extensive irrigation systems.

Today, with desalination methods, water accumulation
systems, and irrigation methods, Israel is pioneering in
making a desert productive. Today, plants are growing
experimentally in the Dead Sea area where no agriculture
ever occurred previously in the history of man.

HEBREW PRINTING

He giveth power to the faint;
And to him who hath no might
He increaseth strength.

Isaiah 40:29

Czechoslovakia: 1967
Jewish Publishing
Company Insignia

THIS stamp is an amazing memento. It is a Judaica item published by an antireligious country, based on material rescued and salvaged by an anti-Semitic state actively trying to exterminate all Jews; and it was delayed from its scheduled issue date (and almost not issued at all) by anti-Zionism.

The design of the stamp consists primarily of the imprint of a Jewish family-owned printing enterprise (Gersoniden) dating back to 1530. The inscription in Hebrew is a part of the original Gersoniden design; it includes a quotation from Isaiah.

The stamp is one of a set of six issued to mark the thousand-year-old history of the Jewish community` in Czechoslovakia. That Jewish history would be emphasized in any way in a country under Soviet influence at a time when the USSR was methodically strangling Jewish expression is in itself amazing.

All six stamps in the set owe their motif to the Nazis. It was part of the Nazi plan to rescue some Jewish relics

153

and display them in a Jewish museum. They expected to exterminate all evidence of the Jews and wanted some reminder for posterity.

A complication that interfered with the scheduled issue date was the 1967 war between Israel and the Arab states. The Communist countries supported the Arab states during and after that war, and they were sensitive to Arab denunciation of sentiment expressed in this stamp set and, particularly, this stamp, which they said encouraged Zionism.

TAKE COURAGE

*They helped every one his
    neighbor;
And every one said to his
    brother:
'Be of good courage.'*

Isaiah 41:6

IN the instance of commemorating the International Cooperation Year, an outgrowth of the United Nations de-
liberations, Israel issued a multilanguage stamp with a
symbolic design. The biblical connection is not in the
stamp but elsewhere on the envelope, which philatelists
refer to as a "cover." Because the stamp was cancelled on
the day that it was first available for postage usage, it is
known as a "first-day cover." In fact, this cover is so
identified in both Hebrew and French in the hexagon in
the upper left-hand corner.

Israel: 1965
International Cooperation Year

THE TORAH SCROLL

Israel: 1967
Rosh Hashana 5728

... for his righteousness' sake; he will magnify the law, and make it honorable.

Isaiah 42:21

THE Torah scroll pictured on this Israeli stamp is without question identical to all other Torah scrolls, despite the fact that it is handwritten. The reverence felt toward the Torah required that it not be changed even in any small way down through the ages. Painstaking rabbinic details had to be scrupulously followed at all stages of its production. The copying of a Torah is considered an act of religious worship to be engaged in, only by a pious man. An ordinary mistake could be erased, but if ever God's name was written with error, the entire parchment sheet had to be destroyed.

As a means of preventing errors from creeping in during the calligraphy, a procedure known as the "Masora" was instituted. It consists of a system of cross reference tables and lists which are placed in various places on the Torah page, including around the initial words of a section and written in tiny letters to form a kind of decoration.

157

THE STRAITS
OF TIRAN

When thou passest through
* the waters, I will be with*
* thee,*
And through the rivers, they
* shall not overflow thee;*
When thou walkest through
* the fire, thou shalt not be*
* burned,*
Neither shall the flame
* kindle upon thee.*
For I am the Lord thy
* God, . . .*

Isaiah 43:2-3

Israel: 1967
Victory in the Six-Day War
The Straits of Tiran

FREEDOM of navigation through international water-
ways has not always been permitted Israel. Egypt has
not allowed Israeli boats to make use of the Suez Canal.
When in 1964 in addition, Egypt declared Israel's only
other waterway, the Straits of Tiran, closed to Israeli
shipping and cargoes, a naval blockade was thereby im-
plemented. Israel took this as an act of war, seen against
the background of troop deployment of the surrounding
Arab states as well as their proclaimed belligerency. The
celebrated Six-Day War in which Israel emerged victori-
ously was the result. To mark her triumph, Israel issued
a set of three stamps honoring her armed forces. One
features the emblem of the Israeli military forces. The
other two portray views of two prime military objectives,
the Old City of Jerusalem and the Strait of Tiran. By
representing an Israeli ship in the Tiran Strait, this stamp
symbolizes freedom of navigation for Israel.

158

THE ISRAEL
MERCHANT
MARINE

Israel: 1958
Honoring Merchant Marine

Art thou not it that
dried up the sea,
The waters of the great
deep;
That made the depths of
the sea a way
For the redeemed to
pass over?

Isaiah 51:10

THERE is an ancient and recurrent myth that appears almost universally in folk legend dealing with the struggle between the godhead(s) and a rebellious dragon(s) of the nether waters. Typically, the dragon monster who controls the waters is subdued by god(s) or god-forces at the beginning of the year to prevent the flooding of the earth. Obviously there are many variant versions.

Some mythologists read references to Leviathan in Israelite folklore as an equivalent myth. Some also suggest that allusions to the same primordial struggle is evidenced in the Bible in passages such as this fragment from Isaiah and in some of the Psalms (74:13–14, 89: 9–10, and 93) and in some sections of Job (7:12 and 26: 12–13).

THE ETERNAL CITY

Awake, awake
Stand up, O Jerusalem,
Thou hast drunk at the hand of
the Lord
The cup of His fury;
Thou hast drunken the beaker,
even the cup of staggering,
And drained it.

Isaiah 51:17

Israel: 1968
Festival Stamps

JERUSALEM is a city with deep religious importance for three major religions, Judaism, Christianity, and Mohammedanism. Although it is called the eternal city, it is not the oldest city even in that area. Called the city of peace, it has probably experienced more war, and possibly been destroyed more times than any other city.

Prior to the biblical record, particularly King David's capture of the city from the Jebusites, a Canaanite clan, very little is known about the city with certainty. It is known to have existed early in the fourteenth century B.C.E. from written records showing correspondence with Egypt.

Since David's time, Jews have always lived in Jerusalem. Even when the city was torn down time and again, some Jews continued to live there, if only to lament the loss of the Temple and the holy city.

The biblical record indicated that until David captured the city, the northern and southern parts of the Hebrew kingdom could not be united. Having made it his capital and the permanent home of the Holy Ark, it became for all time the focal point of Judaism. On every holiday, particularly Passover, the words "next year in Jerusalem" were recited wherever Jews were found.

THE SYNAGOGUE

Surinam: 1968
Commemorates first
Jewish settlement
in Dutch Guiana

. . . For my house shall be called
A house of prayer for all peoples.

Isaiah 56:7

THE Jewish community of Surinam is the oldest permanent Jewish settlement in the Western Hemisphere. A Dutch colony, with large sugar and rice plantations worked by African slaves, it became a haven for Jews fleeing the Portuguese Inquisition.

The stamp depicts the Joden Savanne Synagogue (Jewish Savannah Synagogue), which dates back to the 1600's and is currently being restored. Along with two other stamps, it was issued to mark the renovation and restoration of the 439-tombstone Jewish cemetery of Savannah.

THE WALLS OF JERUSALEM

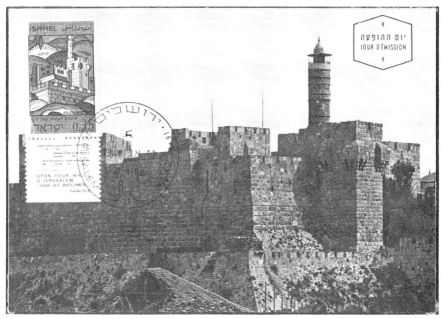

I have set watchmen
Upon thy walls, O Jerusalem,
They shall never hold their peace
Day nor night:
'Ye that are the Lord's
   remembrancers,

Take ye no rest,
And give Him no rest,
Till He establish, and till He
   make Jerusalem
A praise in the earth.'

Isaiah 62:6-7

THIS stamp with the attached tab is affixed to a maximum card which typically reproduces the motif of the stamp. In this instance the design consists of the Citadel of David and a portion of the wall of the Old City of Jerusalem. Archeological proof of the exact location of the complete original walls that surrounded the city are not available. The walls were demolished and rebuilt for purposes of expansion, and, sometimes, in the many battles that took place there, so that it is unclear as to when and which portions were built and rebuilt.

JERUSALEM—THE GOLDEN

Rejoice ye with Jerusalem,
And be glad with her, all ye that
*   love her;*
Rejoice for joy with her,
All ye that mourn for her; . . .

                    Isaiah 66:10

Israel: 1968

T HE unsuspecting visitor to Jerusalem is astonished to discover a windmill standing in the middle of the busy city. It served as an observation post throughout the siege of Jerusalem during the 1948 War of Independence, when the area which housed Jewish residents was isolated by Arabs for months but never captured. The British philanthropist Moses Montefiore is credited with its construction, so as to serve the Jewish community that had begun to proliferate in the area outside the walls of the Old City. The windmill had its top destroyed by the British authorities during the Mandate period when they were experiencing difficulty maintaining control. That project was promptly unofficially named "Operation Don Quixote" by the area residents.

163

THE PROPHET
JEREMIAH

Vatican: 1964
Celebration of Michelangelo's
400-Year Anniversary
"Jeremiah" by Michelangelo

*Cursed be the day wherein I was born: let not the day
wherein my mother bore me be blessed,*
*Cursed be the man who brought tidings to my father,
saying,*
'A man child is born to thee'; making him very glad.
*And let that man be as the cities which the Lord over-
threw and repented not: and let him hear the cry in
the morning, and the shouting at noontide;*
*Because he slew me not from the womb; or that my
mother might have been my grave, and her womb to
be always pregnant with me.*
*Wherefore came I forth out of the womb to see labor and
sorrow, that my days should be consumed with shame?*

Jeremiah 20:14-18

T HE unpopular proclamations of Jeremiah alienated
almost everyone. He was denounced by his relatives; the
royal family was infuriated at him, the king at one point
deliberately cutting off sections of Jeremiah's writings
from a scroll and feeding them to a fire. The priests,
angered time and again, on one occasion had him beaten

and hung in stocks. He was jailed and often faced death. Tradition has it that he was finally put to death by his fellow Jewish exiles in Egypt when they could no longer put up with him. Despite all the misery he felt, he persisted in his message that the end of the state would not mean the end of the covenant.

His personal grief and his intense as well as bitter mourning regarding the pending doom he forsaw would befall the nation, earned him the lasting reputation of a cryer of lamentations.

The English word "jeremiad", which means a woeful or bitter tirade, a lament, is a part of the semantic heritage he leaves us. The ethical heritage is too immense to capture in one word.

THE PROPHET OF DOOM

Italy: 1961
"Jeremiah" by
Michelangelo

And seek the peace of the city
whither I have caused you to be
carried away captive, and pray
unto the Lord for it; for in the
peace thereof shall ye have peace.

Jeremiah 29:7

EXPECTING the destruction of the Jewish state, and even anticipating the desolation of the Holy City and the Temple, Jeremiah looked to the exile as the only way the remnant might survive as observant Jews. However, his pleas that the people embrace a life in foreign lands, even so far as to pray for the peace of their captors, was an unthinkable idea in his time. Yet it was, indeed, this remnant in exile that survived and maintained the long chain of Jewish tradition.

Even while Jeremiah was prophesying the destruction of the land, and particularly at a time when he was imprisoned, the prophet pointedly purchased some land in the Jewish state, thereby demonstrating his faith in its ultimate restoration.

THE BIRTH OF ZIONISM

Israel: 1967   50th Anniversary of the Balfour Declaration

And there is hope for thy future, saith the Lord;
And thy children shall return to their own border.

Jeremiah 31:16

THE British government, as the Mandate power over Palestine and on behalf of the League of Nations, gave political sanction to the growing Zionist movement in 1917. The document of recognition of its aims was in the form of a letter from the British Foreign Minister Lord Arthur James Balfour addressed to Lord Rothschild, one of many outstanding English Zionists who, along with Dr. Chaim Weizmann and others, were diligently working toward the goal of a national home for Jews in Palestine.

Unfortunately, the language of diplomacy in which the Balfour Declaration was couched led to many disappointments and problems later on. In contrast, the simple declaration of the prophet Jeremiah reminds the world of the pact between the Jewish people and God: ". . . and thy children shall return to their own country."

THE LAMENT OF JERUSALEM

Oman
"Jeremiah Lamenting the Destruction of Jerusalem"
by Rembrandt

Thus saith the Lord, the God of Israel: Go, and speak to Zedekiah, king of Judah, and tell him: Thus saith the Lord: Behold, I will give this city into the hand of the king of Babylon, and he shall burn it with fire; . . .

Jeremiah 34:2

JEWISH folk tales take revenge on the Babylonian King Nebuchadnezzer for his act of destroying Jerusalem and the Temple. The stories tell how the king feared punishment for these deeds, but that his priests consoled him on the basis that Judea was captured not through the king's strength, but through the Jews' wickedness.

There is also the biblical account of how Nebuchadnezzar's fears spilled over into his dreams and how, in one episode, he demanded to know the meaning of one of the dreams which, however, he would not recall. The prophet Daniel was then found and he told the king that he saw in his dream a giant with a head of gold, hands of silver, body of brass and feet of clay; and that a stone was thrown at the giant shattering him in pieces.

Daniel interpreted the dream: the king was the monstrous giant, as all anyone can dream of is himself. Daniel did not also say, but he knew, that the dream told that Nebuchadnezzer was doomed to a horrible punishment. The king would develop the delusion that he became an ox, and would be driven by men into the fields to graze. While the biblical narrative supplies most of the above information, it is expanded upon in the folklore.

THE PROPHET EZEKIEL

*... if a man is just, and do that
which is lawful and right, and
hath not eaten upon the
mountains, neither hath lifted up
his eyes to the idols of the house of
Israel, neither hath defiled his
neighbor's wife ... and hath not
wronged any, hath taken naught
by robbery, hath given his bread
to the hungry ... hath executed
true justice between man and
man .... he is just, he shall
surely live, saith the Lord God.*

Ezekiel 18:5-9

D ESPITE his dramatic voicing of the doom that was
imminent, and cataleptic fits that might suddenly cut off
his speech, Ezekiel was consulted by the elders of the
people for his respected advice. The exile that had been
forecast by Jeremiah had come to pass, and prophets
were vindicated.

With Jerusalem and the Temple destroyed, the nation
would soon be dissipated and lost in oblivion as happened to all other dispersed peoples. Ezekiel helped to
circumvent this by giving a new direction to Israel—to
continue not as a nation, but rather as an ecclesiastical
organization. The idea of individual conscience, first
stated by Jeremiah, was also developed by him, and
became his great message. Ezekiel was the first prophet
who spoke while in exile. He lived in a Babylonian village named Tel Aviv.

FREEDOM FROM HUNGER

Israel: 1963
Freedom From Hunger

*. . . and I will call for the
corn, and will increase it, and
lay no famine upon you.*

Ezekiel 36:29

IN cooperation with the United Nations Food and Agricultural Organization (F.A.O.) campaign for a movement towards "Freedom from Hunger," many countries issued commemorative stamps. Israel publicized the campaign with its own design showing an outstretched hand offering food to a bird and an attached tab quotation from Ezekiel in French and Hebrew.

171

THE PROPHET JOEL

Brazil: 1958
Centennial of the Church
of Bom Jesus do Matosinhos

*The word of the Lord that came
to Joel the son of Pethuel.*

Joel 1:1

IN a small village in Brazil are some of the world's finest examples of baroque architecture and sculpture. It is amazing that the artist who created this little-seen work was so badly crippled that he had to have his chisel strapped to his hand and wrist. Aleijadinho (Little Cripple), as the unschooled Antonio Lisboa came to be called, was a mulatto whose father was a Portuguese construction foreman and whose mother was a Negro slave. He never traveled more than fifty miles from his birthplace and most of what he learned about art was on his own. This despite a progressive painful illness that disfigured him. Ultimately, he could not even walk and had to be carried everywhere. He finally became blind and paralyzed. The head of the prophet Joel shown on this stamp, is from a full statue which was the artist's last project. It consisted of a group of twelve biblical Prophets and stands in the courtyard of the Church of Bom Jesus do Matosinhos in the village of Ouro Preto.

Agriculture is the primary strength of the Brazilian economy. However, it frequently is subject to severe destruction by invading locusts. The prophet Joel as the patron saint of agriculture in Brazil is featured on this stamp.

172

THE PROPHECY OF JOEL

Italy: 1961
"Joel" by
Michelangelo

*That which the palmerworm
hath left hath the locust eaten;
and that which the locust hath
left hath the cankerworm eaten;
and that which the cankerworm
hath left hath the caterpillar
eaten.*

Joel 1:4

THE immediate event that prompted Joel to call upon the people to repent their ways was an exceptionally severe plague of locusts followed by extended drought and famine. Interpreters of the Bible and its events originally believed that the locusts spoken of in the Book of Joel were symbols and not real. Later writers now believe otherwise. They agree with the descriptions of Joel that indeed a plague of locusts cause darkness, make a fearsome noise, seem somehow to resemble horses, are fantastically destructive, advance irresistably, leaving any region they have ravaged looking as though it had been burnt out afterwards. Joel called the endless invading locusts "the northern army": . . . "a nation is come up upon my land, strong and without number, whose teeth are the teeth of the lion. . . ."

JOEL THE PROPHET

And it shall come to pass in that day, that the mountains shall drop down new wine, and the hills shall flow with milk, and all the rivers of Judah shall flow with waters, and a fountain shall come forth of the house of the Lord, and shall water the valley of Shittim.

Joel 4:18

Vatican: 1964
Celebration of Michelangelo's
400-Year Anniversary
"Joel" by Michelangelo

T HE Book of Joel is clearly composed of two contrasting sections. The first part conveys a description of the calamity (plague of locusts) and relates it to the sinful ways of the people, with further dire results to follow if they do not repent. In the second section, there is the implication that the people have obeyed the injunctions Joel conveys from God and the list of calamities is replaced by a list of blessings. Nor is this dichotomy found only in Joel. Most of the prophets warn of future dangers, and also promise peace and plenty. How is one to know if their prophesy would hold true?

Jewish folklore has a ready answer. False prophets could never be believed. Their motives were personal, and their words reflected that instead of God's word. However, even the true prophet could deliver a prophesy that might not be fulfilled. Never was this likely to be so with prophecies of peace and plenty. Prophecies of misfortune could always be averted simply by repentance of the listeners.

174

THE WISDOM
OF AMOS

And I will plant them upon
    their land,
And they shall no more be
    plucked up
Out of their land which I have
    given them,
Saith the Lord, thy God.

Amos 9:15

Israel: 1958
Convention Center·
Jerusalem

AMOS is one of twelve prophets whose works have
survived only in fragmentary form. When the kingdoms
of Israel and Judah were conquered and dispersed, much
of the written legacy of the prophets was destroyed and
lost. Because what has survived for later generations to
see is so little, it is sometimes difficult to establish when
each of these twelve lived, or to know much about their
personal lives. They are known collectively as the Minor
Prophets. However, the term refers to the small quantity
of their work which has survived and not to its lack of
quality or importance. In Hebrew, they are not even re-
ferred to as minor prophets, but as "The Twelve." In
addition to Amos, they are (listed alphabetically here,
but not in the Bible) Habakkuk, Haggai, Hosea, Joel,
Jonah, Malachi, Micah, Nahum, Obadiah, Zechariah,
Zephaniah. The three major prophets are Isaiah, Jeremiah, and Ezekiel.

175

JONAH THE PROPHET

*Now the word of the Lord came
unto Jonah the son of Amittai,
saying, 'Arise, go to Nineveh,
that great city, and cry against it;
for their wickedness is come up
before me.'*

Italy: 1961
"Jonah" by
Michelangelo

Jonah 1:1-2

SALVATION or wisdom brought to a people by a human with the form of a fish is a theme oft-repeated in mankind's legends and in religious history. In the story of Jonah a man who is swallowed by a great fish carries God's word to a sinful people. There are other versions as well among the ancients. One tells of Oannes whose whole body was that of a large fish, but under whose fish head was a man's head and a man's feet joined the tail. He brought learning to the inhabitants of Chaldea. He taught them to build cities and to make laws and to understand geometry, and he civilized their lives. He lived with them by day but returned to the sea at night. Less dramatic is the story of the Hindu redeemer Vishnu who was expelled from the mouth of a fish in his first incarnation. In this same context it is interesting to note that the Greek name for Jesus (IXOYE) means "a fish," and that early Christians used a fish as a symbol of Christ.

THE PROPHET JONAH

But the Lord hurled a great wind into the sea, and there was a mighty tempest in the sea, so that the ship was like to be broken.

Jonah 1:4

Israel: 1963
Festival Stamps

THE story of Jonah is essentially a description of the broadening of the Jewish religion to a universal religion. God is presented not as just the God of the Hebrews, but as the God of all mankind. Any people that repents its ways and embraces Him finds salvation.

Jonah symbolizes the struggle in this concept. He refuses to go to Nineveh to carry God's word, and has to be compelled to do so. The entire people do repent (perhaps a greater miracle than the story of the great fish swallowing Jonah and casting him up alive three days later) and are saved. However, the available historical and archeological data do not confirm any evidence of conversion of the Ninevites. The Book of Jonah marks a significant milestone in the Bible. In it an anonymous author, imbued with the spirit of prophetic idealism, challenges his people in this poetic story to understand a more mature concept of the nature of God. God is the God of all, with equal moral requirements and equal solicitude for all.

177

JONAH AND
THE WHALE

*And the Lord prepared a
great fish to swallow up
Jonah; and Jonah was in the
belly of the fish three days
and three nights.*

Jonah 2:1

Israel: 1963
Festival Stamps

THE mythical elements in the Book of Jonah were
especially difficult to account for by persons who believed
the Bible to be literal truth—an historical statement of
fact. One interpretation given to "explain" the great fish
which carried Jonah in its bowels, was that he was really
in a boat which had a fish shape. (Another variation was
that it was a boat which was named "Great Fish".) Even
more complicated was the explanation of at least one
writer who decided that it was a great fish, but dead which
the Lord provided to carry Jonah, thereby he was not
disintegrated by its digestive juices.

Allegorical explanations were easier. An example of
this being that Jonah was symbolic of the nation of Israel, with Babylon represented by the whale. Another
view ascribes the story as a residual concern with the
phenomena of the solar eclipse. Jonah is swallowed and
later disgorged as is the sun during an eclipse.

JONAH FEELS DISCREDITED

. . . and the sun beat upon the head of Jonah, that he fainted, and requested for himself that he might die. . . .

Jonah 4:8

Pᴀʀᴀʟʟᴇʟs to the story of Jonah can be found in all parts of the world. Egyptian lore tells of a shipwrecked traveler carried to shore by a serpent which swallowed him. The natives of Windesi in northern New Guinea tell a story of five men in a canoe swallowed by a whale who kept themselves alive by eating slices of its innards cooked over a fire made by burning the canoe.

A tale from India concerns a traveler who disobeyed his mother and was found out by selecting lots aboard a ship, which could not proceed until he was cast overboard. It is not clear as to which of the many parallel tales is the antecedent of the biblical story and which, if any, are variants of it. None, however, have the emphatic prophetic spirit of the writer or writers of the story of Jonah which clearly teaches that one God is over all.

179

THE WISDOM OF MICAH

Russia: 1960

And he shall judge among many peoples, and rebuke strong nations afar off; and they shall beat their swords into plowshares, and their spears into pruning hooks; nation shall not lift up a sword against nation, neither shall they learn war anymore.

Micah 4:3

THE vision of Micah and the vision of Isaiah are almost identical. Nor is this the only example of parallel to identical phrases and passages in the writings of Micah and Isaiah. Obviously scholars have subsequently attempted to explain the duplication. Some scholars contend that Micah was younger than Isaiah and had heard him prophesy (or heard his prophecies) and quoted him. Others claim that it is Isaiah who quotes Micah. There is a third point of view that holds to the opinion that both are quoting from an older prophesy. Still another point of view states that the words are those of an unknown sage which later compilers of the Bible placed in the book in different ways; one crediting Isaiah and another ascribing the words to Micah.

THE MESSAGE
OF MICAH

Israel: 1960
World Refugee Year

*Every man shall
sit under his
vine and fig tree and none
shall make him afraid.*

Micah 4:4

W HEREAS both Micah and Isaiah talk in almost identical words about converting "swords into plowshares," there is one verse found in Micah that is not in the vision of Isaiah. In Micah, "every man . . . sit[s] under his vine and fig tree, . . ." which probably reflects Micah's rural origin and loyalty.

It is clear that Micah preached in the time of King Hezekiah, during the period that Isaiah also spoke God's word. While they were contemporaries, their backgrounds were very different. Isaiah came from a well-known upper-class family and was a native of the great city Jerusalem. Micah is identified as the Morashtite (coming from the village of Moresheth-Gath) instead of by his father's name. The implication is that his family is not well known and that he is of humble birth.

FEASTS OF ISRAEL

Israel: 1950
High Holidays

Behold upon the mountains
  the feet of him
That bringeth good tidings,
  that announceth peace!
Keep thy feasts, O Judah,
Perform thy vows;
For the wicked shall no
  more pass through thee;
He is utterly cut off.

Nahum 2:1

ARTHUR SZYK, the designer of this stamp from Israel, was responsible for what the *London Times,* in 1940, called the most costly book in the world. Only two hundred forty copies were printed, and sold for approximately five hundred dollars each. The book was the illuminated Passover Haggadah which tells the story of the Exodus, and is used during the Passover holiday ceremony. The art of hand illumination, which died with the invention of the printing press, was revived by Szyk who became the master practitioner of the modern miniature. Illumination is interwoven decoratively with the written text of the book using fine details and myriad

182

colors. It quickly became too costly and was replaced with illustrations which are graphic expressions of a particular part of a book.

Szyk was born in June, 1894, in Lodz, Poland, which was then part of Czarist Russia. He was given an intensive Jewish education in a cheder (a Jewish school) which was typical for that time. His drawings in the margins of his books showed such craftsmanship that the rabbi in charge of his school urged that he be given art training. At age fifteen, he was sent to Paris to study art. His work has hung in the White House in Washington and in the royal residence in Britain.

THE PROPHET NAHUM

Brazil: 1964
"Nahum" by Lisboa

And it shall come to pass, that
*   all they that look upon thee*
Shall flee from thee,
And say: 'Nineveh is laid waste;
Who will bemoan her? . . .'

Nahum 3:7

A CAREFUL analysis of the Book of Nahum gives us an inkling of how issues of authorship can sometimes be determined by scholars. The book consists of an actual prophesy or vision fortelling the destruction of the Assyrian city of Nineveh. However, the first ten verses compose an alphabetic acrostic poem. (e.g., the first line begins with the letter "A," the second line begins with "B," the third with "C," etc.) This is hardly in keeping with the mood, tone, and descriptions of the poetry of Chapters 2 and 3. Moreover, place names are mentioned in the acrostic poem which are not suitable to the theme of the fall of Nineveh. From this evidence, critical scholars conclude that the prologue section was added on to Nahum's oracle.

THE PROPHET ZECHARIAH

*Return to Me, says the Lord of
Hosts, and I will return to you.*

Zechariah 1:3

Italy: 1961
"Zechariah" by
Michelangelo

EACH prophet clearly had his own style of preaching. Zechariah, who spoke in prose where most of his predecessors used poetry, did not present himself as in direct communication with God. His divine authority came through angels who explained God's wishes to him, and his visions had a dreamlike quality.

As powerful as the words of any single prophet may be, the combined teachings of all the prophets are so forceful that they form the basis for an ethical life-style that remains an ideal still being sought by mankind. No matter what land or period of history, the voice of the Hebrew prophets continues to be heard.

This is the essence of a story from Jewish folklore about Zechariah: When the Assyrian king Nebuchadnezzar and his soldiers entered the Temple in Jerusalem, the king saw blood seething on one of the stones of the floor. Upon his orders the stone was washed and scoured repeatedly and finally replaced with another stone, but always the blood reappeared. Finally the king demanded to know whose blood was this. He learned it was the blood of the prophet Zechariah. Angered at his pronouncements of doom, the people had stoned him on that spot in the Temple, and his blood still refused to stop flowing.

185

THE VISION OF ZECHARIAH

Israel: 1948
Rosh Hashana

I raised my eyes again and looked; and lo, there was a flying scroll.

Zechariah 5:1

T HE design on this Israeli stamp is identified with the words of Zechariah, who described a vision of a flying scroll which would expose the bearers of false witness and thieves by entering and consuming the house in which they lived. It has other meanings as well. The design is known to be an oval seal which was used to mark properties of the king that were taken in tax collections and paid in oil or wine. The pottery receptacles for storing the fluids were marked not only with the flying scroll, but also with the inscription "for the king."

186

"THESE I REMEMBER"

Israel: 1962
Heroes and
Martyrs Day

These I remember, and pour out
my soul within me,
How I passed on with the throng,
and led them to the house of
God
With the voice of joy and praise,
a multitude keeping holyday.

Psalms 42:5

T HE Book of Psalms is recognized as having five sections which traditional thinkers hold to be parallel to the Five Books of Moses. Psalm 42 is the first of the second section, and begins with the words "To the chief musician . . . for the sons of Korah." In fact, this same reference to the sons of Korah is found at the start of many other Psalms. It is likely that the sons of Korah were Levites who comprised a Temple choir. These were probably descendents of the Korah who was the leader of a rebellion against Moses and who was swallowed by the earth for his troublemaking (Numbers 16). Despite the description that Korah and his cohorts and all their households were thus punished, the Bible later tells us that not all the children of Korah died (Numbers 26).

This striking Israeli stamp recalls the death of innocents. Over six million Jews were annihilated in Hitler's genocidal scheme. This stamp is in memory of their struggles and death in that holocaust.

HEROES OF ISRAEL

These I remember, and pour out
my soul within me,
How I passed on with the throng,
and led them to the house of
God
With the voice of joy and praise,
a multitude keeping holyday.

Psalms 42:5

Israel: 1968
Warsaw Ghetto Uprising

IN May 1943, the arresting words "The Jewish Living Quarters In Warsaw Exists No Longer" appeared on the cover of a report sent to Hitler by the Nazi General who demolished the Warsaw Ghetto. It should have been a simple task to raze the ghetto buildings and exterminate its Jewish inhabitants. However, the Jews having decided they had no chance for survival dedicated themselves to giving up their lives as dearly as possible. Against the mechanized German military forces, the outnumbered, undernourished, and barely armed Jews fought so fiercely with home-made weapons, that the German commander General Strupp wrote in his diary "Those Jews know how to die gloriously. Even I have to admit it." For an unbelievable forty-four days the battle raged, with thousands of Nazi stormtroopers also dying in the uneven battle that finally ended with the leveling of the ghetto.

The design of this stamp depicts a ghetto fighter. It is

taken from a monument by Nathan Rappaport on the site of the ghetto, and depicts a group of heroic ghetto fighters. The Polish government issued a stamp showing the entire monument by Rappaport, in commemorating the twentieth anniversary of the Warsaw Ghetto uprising. This Israeli stamp singled out one figure from that monument for its design.

THE MARTYRS OF ISRAEL

Israel: 1968
For Those Who Died Resisting
Foreign Rule

Nay, but for Thy sake are we
  killed all the day;
We are accounted as sheep for the
  slaughter.

Psalms 44:23

THE death of her soldiers is a heavy loss for Israel to bear and they are recalled to memory time and again on her stamps. Particularly fitting is this verse from Psalms on a stamp dedicated to those who gave their lives resisting invasions.

While the design of the stamp is symbolic, a candle and prison windows, there is little question as to the meaning of the candle. It is a Yizkor candle which in Jewish religious tradition represents the belief in the immortality of the soul. This is the same motif that the stamp designer Yaakov Zim utilized in his earlier stamp showing six lit candles memorializing the death of the six million Jews killed by Hitler. While a large majority of Jews believed in the immortality of the soul, some rejected this idea as far back as the Sadducees in the days of the Second Temple. But even where immortality of the soul was accepted, there was a doctrinal difference between those who believed the tomb became the abode of the soul, and those who held to the idea that all the souls gathered in a common abode after death.

190

THE BLOWING OF
THE SHOFAR

Blow up the horn at the new moon, in the time appointed, on our solemn feast day.

Psalms 81:4

Israel: 1955
Festival Stamps

T HE musical instrument shown on this stamp is a shofar which is fashioned from a ram's horn. It is, today, inextricably connected with the Rosh Hashana festival (Jewish New Year) and is sounded at the close of worship on that holy day; but it predates the time when the holiday was named Rosh Hashana—when it was known as the day of the blowing of the shofar (Yom T'ruah).

The shofar was used in times past not only at religious ceremonies, but to declare war, to announce proclamations to the people, and to intimidate the enemy. Along with shouts from the people and blasts on trumpets, the sound of the shofar was part of the tumultous ceremony associated with bringing down the walls of Jericho.

The Bible speaks of the blowing of the shofar as a method of beseeching God to remember man. A folk belief mantains that the shofar is blown on the New Year to confuse Satan and thereby prevent him from bringing charges against people on Judgment Day.

191

THE PSALMIST SPEAKS

Grenada: 1969
Apollo XI Moonshot

*It shall be established for ever as
the moon;
And be steadfast as the witness
in the sky.*

Selah.

Psalms 89:38

GRENADA, which was a British colony, has been a
self-governing state within the British Commonwealth
since 1967. Located in the Windward Islands of the West
Indies, it is only 133 square miles and consists of a
number of islands including, primarily, Grenada Island

and the southern Grenadines. Prior to the status of "associated statehood," all of Grenada's stamps pictured local scenes or the British royal family—sometimes both. With independence in 1967, the themes of its stamps took on the broadest possible range of subjects including heart, cornea, lung and kidney transplants; paintings by Winston Churchill; Olympic gold-medal winners; and of course moon exploration.

While these stamps from Grenada quote from the Psalms in association with man's exploration of the moon, they are not alone in that association. When the astronauts from the United States landed on the moon, one of a number of souvenirs they left there to mark the event was a disc with a quotation from Psalms:

When I behold Your heavens . . .
The moon and the stars which You have formed
What is man that You should be mindful of him? . . .
You have made him little less than the angels,
And crowned him with glory and honor.
You have given him rule over the works of your
hands, putting all things under his feet. . . ."

Psalms 8:4-7

PEACE OF JERUSALEM

Israel: 1968

Pray for the peace of Jerusalem;
May they prosper that love thee.

Psalms 122:6

T HE English word "psalm" comes from the Greek and implies instrumental music. This is in keeping with the fact that many of the Psalms were sung or recited by the Levites accompanied by instruments. In Hebrew, however, they are called *T'hillim* which is translated as "songs of praise." The Book of Psalms, unlike most of the rest of the Bible, consists of works wherein individuals address their feelings to God. In most of the Bible it is the people Israel who are being addressed, generally by the prophets or by God. In the Psalms, the words of thanks or pleas for help permit the people to express to God their feelings of hurt or happiness.

ANCIENT MUSICAL INSTRUMENTS

Israel: 1955-56

*Praise Him with the psaltery
and harp.*

Psalms 150:3

MARKING the Jewish New Year in 1955, and again in 1956, Israel issued seven different stamps depicting ancient musical instruments mentioned in the Bible. The harp (shown on the 250 pruta stamp) and the psaltery which is also sometimes called a lyre (shown on the 30 pruta stamp) are deservedly a part of that set. Of the approximately twenty different instruments mentioned in the Bible, the psaltery and the harp were favorites among the Jews. Evidence based on analysis of ancient literatures and archeological findings seems to indicate that they were used to accompany songs primarily of a joyous nature. It is certain they were not used on occasions of mourning (see Psalms 137:2). None of the ancient musical instruments were used to play melodies. Rather they were percussive and emphasized the rhythm and tempo of the dancers or singers.

PRAISE THE LORD

Israel: 1955
Festival Stamps

Praise Him upon the timbrel.
Praise Him upon the high
sounding cymbals.

Psalms 150:4-5

THE Book of Psalms is a book of poetry which is unique in ancient literatures. Unlike epic poems which spoke of the grandeur of a nation by glorification of a hero, this was poetry that expressed the inner feelings of the individual at a time when people were not schooled to consider inner moods as important enough for permanent literary purposes.

A classification of the Psalms is difficult because the individual psalms are often so different from one another. However, some major groupings can be distinguished as follows: hymns extolling God, communal laments, individual laments, communal songs of thanksgiving, individual giving of thanks, oracular psalms, royal psalms, and wisdom psalms.

The Book of Psalms has particular appeal for the Christians. More than any other scripture, parts of it are quoted in the New Testament. Its deep influence on Christian religious values is marked. In contrast, later generations of Jews gave their most profound attention to the Law—and Five Books of Moses.

196

THE WISDOM OF THE TORAH

Israel: 1967
Festival Stamps
5728

*Length of days is in her right
hand; and in her left hand riches
and honour.*

Proverbs 3:16

T HERE are two separate and unrelated biblical quotations on this stamp from Israel. The stamp is one of a set of five issued to mark the New Year festival 5728 (1967) and showing designs of ancient Torahs. On the Torah (scroll inscribed with the five Books of Moses) itself are the words, "land of flowing milk and honey." On the attached tab is the inscription from Proverbs. To find the two together is interesting because of all the biblical books, Proverbs particularly strikes a tone markedly different from the Torah. Nothing written in Proverbs is stated as a law or commandment. Nor did the authors present themselves as God's prophets, priests, or delegates. What they offered was wisdom. Moreover, the content of their wisdom is nonsectarian, and offers practical counsel to all, not only to the people of Israel. In fact the word "Israel" does not appear at all, whereas the word "man" (mankind) occurs over thirty times. Given the tone of a universality of Proverbs, the combination on one stamp with the "sectarian" Torah theme is unexpected.

197

THE BOOK OF PROVERBS

Israel: 1967
Festival Stamps 5728

*Her ways are ways of
pleasantness, and all her paths
are peace.*

Proverbs 3:17

J EREMIAH says that there are three classes of teachers
in Israel (Jeremiah 18:18): "Instruction shall not perish
from the priest, nor counsel from the wise, nor the word
from the prophet." Ezekiel also differentiates between
the three groups of teachers (Ezekiel 7:26) when he
talks of the vision of the prophet; instruction from the
priest; and counsel from the elders. It was the prophets'
role to carry divine messages to the people, the priests'
role to be the agent for instructing the people in the
practices of ritual and response to their God; whereas
the "elders" or the "wise" gave guidance for the affairs of
everyday living. The latter group had no authority other
than the validity of their teachings. They did not speak in
the name of God. But the literature of their teachings has
also been canonized as was the literature of the prophets
and the priests. It is generally called the Wisdom Literature and typically includes Proverbs, Job, and Ecclesiastes.

THE TREE OF LIFE

Israel: 1967
Festival Stamps 5728

*She is a tree of life to them that
lay hold upon her: and happy is
everyone that retaineth her.*

Proverbs 3:18

T HE implications of this Israeli stamp which pictures a
Torah scroll and quotes from Proverbs, "She is a tree of
life to them that lay hold upon her . . .," is that it is the
Torah which is a tree of life. However, a careful reading
of this portion of proverbs shows that the reference is to
Wisdom, not Torah, as a tree of life. (Note that the
Torah scroll consists only of the Five Books of Moses
and, therefore, does not include Proverbs.) However, so
narrow an understanding misses the significance of Torah
to the Jews. It *is* equated with wisdom. In fact the reading
from the Torah during the worship service is always accompanied by reciting these words from Proverbs at the
close of the reading when the Torah is being returned to
its place in the Ark. It happened that the verses from
Proverbs are recited in their reverse order in the Torah
ritual (Proverbs 3:18, 3:17, 3:16), but the meaning is
unchanged. Interestingly, in the prayers that surround
the Torah reading the emphasis is on God and not Torah.

WONDROUS THINGS

There are three things which
*   are too wonderful for me,*
Yea, four which I know not:
The way of an eagle in the
*   air;*
The way of a serpent upon a
*   rock;*
The way of a ship in the
*   midst of the sea;*
And the way of a man with
*   a young woman.*

Proverbs 30:18-19

Israel: 1958
Honoring the Merchant Marine

To honor her merchant marine, Israel issued a set of four stamps in 1958 which in their design conveyed a brief history of ships associated with Israel. Beginning with a design based on wall drawings in caves explored by archeologists in the Beth Shearim area, the ship shown on the first stamp in the series dates back to biblical times. On the last stamp in the series is a modern-day passenger ship powered by steam turbine and capable of carrying 4000 tons of cargo and over 300 passengers.

The ship shown on this stamp is the "Nirit," a sailing vessel built in 1910, and which, despite its age, was used to bring illegal immigrants to Palestine prior to the proclamation of the State of Israel. Many of the vessels used in this project of bringing in Jewish refugees in violation of the British Mandate authorities, were often not seaworthy, and were always overloaded.

THE GOOD WIFE

*She is like the merchant-
ships;
She bringeth her food from
afar.*

Proverbs 31:14

Taken out of context, it would be impossible to recognize that the Bible verse accompanying this stamp is part of a long glowing tribute to the "good wife". The major portion of the last chapter of Proverbs describes the ideal wife, homemaker, and mother. Beginning with "A woman of valour, who can find? For her price is far above rubies . . .," this section describes in much detail, the attributes of such a woman. In the traditional Jewish home, this poem is recited by the husband-father on the Sabbath eve.

One explanation for concluding the Book of Proverbs with a testimonial to the good wife, may be by way of compensating for the fact that the unfaithful wife is often mentioned throughout Proverbs. This poem which takes the form of an alphabetical acrostic, balances the tone of the book and permits it to end on a positive note.

201

THE PROPHET JOB

Now when Job's three friends heard of all this evil that was come upon him, they came every one from his own place. . . .

Job 2:11

Rwanda: 1967
"Job Visited by His Friends"
by Il Calabrese

THE Book of Job touches every human life insofar as each of us at some point experiences hurt, pain, and suffering. Yet rare is the individual who believes that he deserves that suffering. Unearned happiness and unearned suffering were subjects also in the literature of other ancient peoples. There is a Mesopotamian poem, so similar to the Biblical Job that scholars at times have called it *The Babylonian Job*.

So well written and so intriguing is the Book of Job that there is tremendous interest in it and tremendous differences of opinion as to its essential meaning. One major point of view holds that because of man's finite intellect and nature, there can be no complete comprehension of God by man; and that this is the essence of the Job story. Another viewpoint is that the purpose of the book is served in its flaming dramatic exposition of a problem with no answer. Yet others maintain that the various ideas expressed in the Book of Job point up that there are many solutions, each of which has truth enough to satisfy a given person or generation at some time or place.

The folklore claims that Job was so righteous, except for one flaw, that his name nearly came to be joined to the name of God in prayer, as in God of Abraham, Isaac, and Jacob. Job wavered in his faith and therefore was not rewarded as was Abraham. Witness: Abraham chastised God in His plan to totally destroy S'dom and G'morah: ". . . That be far from thee to do . . . to slay the righteous with the wicked." Job chastised God also, but said, "It is all one; therefore I say, He destroyeth the perfect and the wicked,".

A SONG OF
   LOVE

I am a rose of Sharon,
A lily of the valleys.

Song of Songs 2:1

Israel: 1952
High Holiday Set
Illustrations from
The Song of Songs

The fig-tree putteth forth her
   green figs,
And the vines in blossom give
   forth their fragrance.
Arise, my love, my fair one,
   and come away.

Song of Songs 2:13

O my dove, that art in the clefts of the rock, in the
   covert of the cliff.

Let me see thy countenance, let me hear thy voice;
For sweet is thy voice, and thy countenance is comely.

Song of Songs 2:14

I went down into the garden of nuts,
To look at the green plants of the valley,
To see whether the vine budded,
And the pomegranates were in flower.

Song of Songs 6:11

ARRANGED in numerical value, this set of stamps spells out the acronym for the coming New Year that it commemorates. By enlarging a significant character in the Hebrew biblical text on the bottom of each stamp, the year is identified. The accompanying designs illustrate the text which is a quotation from the Song of Songs.

There is dispute among scholars as to the meaning of this biblical book. Some claim it to be an extraordinarily beautiful love poem. Others see in it religious or historical significance, as well. One point of view describes it as an unsuccessful attempt by King Solomon to woo a beautiful maiden away from her shepherd lover. Others describe it as a love epic describing Solomon and a beautiful shepherdess who develop an intense love for one another that purifies and ennobles both. Another point of view holds that it consists of fragments from the love songs forming part of the wedding ceremonies of the ancient Semitic peoples and still seen today in Syrian wedding rites. An allegorical interpretation sees in the book the love relationship between God and the nation Israel; and as such it is considered particularly sacred despite its frank language and content. The moral lesson is that love, in addition to being the strongest emotion, can also be the holiest.

QUEEN ESTHER
AND HAMAN

*And the king arose in his wrath
from the banquet of wine and
went into the palace garden; but
Haman remained to make request
for his life to Esther the
queen. . . .*

Esther 7:7

IN the painting of the villain, Haman pleading for mercy from Queen Esther, the famous artist Rembrandt portrays the dramatic highlights of the Purim story. Haman, who hates the Jews, plans to kill them all and has chosen the day by casting lots. (The name Purim is thought to be an ancient Persian or Akkadian word meaning "to cast lots.") Esther, who is Jewish, turns the plot against Haman. That this secular tale which contains not a single mention of the name of God, could find its way into a book of sacred writings is surprising. Even more so when the names of the Jewish heroes Mordecai

206

and Esther are recognized as disguised forms of the ancient gods Marduk and Ishtar!

One interpretation of the text suggests that Haman symbolizes not a person, but a destructive force among men; and that Esther and Mordecai are the prototypes of the idealized victims who become victors in the eternal miracle of Jewish survival.

The history of the Jewish people contains many such nearly fatal experiences with a dramatic rescue. Certainly this book of the Bible encouraged many Jews in adverse times.

There are, in fact, innumerable special Purims. Private families, religious congregations, Jewish communities often instituted the observance of a Purim of their own to mark their escape from a fatal threat.

THE HANDWRITING ON THE WALL

In the same hour came forth fingers of a man's hand, and wrote over against the candlestick upon the plaster of the wall of the king's palace; and the king saw the palm of the hand that wrote.

Daniel 5:5

Grenada: 1969
Human Rights
"Belshazzar's Feast" by
Rembrandt

EVEN today, use is still made of the phrase "the handwriting on the wall" to indicate pending disaster. It's origin is the story in the Book of Daniel wherein a mysterious hand appears from nowhere and writes a strange message on the wall. Only Daniel is able to interpret it and he reads it as a warning that the king's days are numbered. That very night the king is killed and the kingdom is divided between the Persians and Medes.

This stamp from Grenada reproduces a painting by Rembrandt whose Hebrew letters are visible within the circle of light in the upper right-hand corner, spelling out the mysterious message "mene, mene, tekel, upharsin." Paradoxically, they can be seen (under a magnifying glass) to read from top to bottom, rather than from right to left as ought to be, in keeping with the Hebrew script. Actually the words are probably Aramaic rather than Hebrew. Speculation as to their meaning includes the notion that they represent the names of weights as though to suggest Belshazzar's kingdom was weighed and found wanting.

THE BOOK OF DANIEL

. . . the king spoke and said to Daniel: 'O Daniel, servant of the living God, is thy God whom thou servest continually, able to deliver thee from the lions?'

Daniel 6:21

Italy: 1961
"Daniel" by
Michelangelo

B IBLICAL authorities are convinced that the purpose of the Book of Daniel is to encourage the Jews to adhere to their faith at a time when observance and belief might falter. A series of stories tells how Daniel and his friends remain faithful to their religion in the face of all sorts of trials and how God invariably rescued and rewarded them. The famous tale of Daniel in the lions den is one such narration.

However, there is much disagreement among these same authorities as to why the Book of Daniel is written largely in Aramaic. It is interesting to note that the Bible experts are able to agree not only on the purpose of the Book of Daniel, but even almost the exact date when it appeared, without reaching a uniform point of view as to the use of Aramaic.

Christianity considers Daniel in a special light: as one of the prophets of the Bible. This is due to the way the writer speaks of the future in a style that is called "apocalyptic." Typically apocalyptic writing "reveals" the future, usually portraying terrible anguish and suffering. God then moves to rescue the suffering ones from their pain.

THE ANGEL GABRIEL

Portugal: 1962
The Angel Gabriel

Yea, while I was speaking in prayer, the man Gabriel, whom I had seen in the vision at the beginning, being caused to fly swiftly, approached close to me about the time of the evening offering. And he made me to understand, and talked with me, and said: 'O Daniel, I am now come forth to make thee skilful of understanding. . . .'

Daniel 9:21-22

DESPITE the extensive belief in angels throughout the ancient world, the Bible moves to an acceptance of angels only slowly. As contact with other cultures increased, the Hebrews became more involved in angelology. Thus, where supernatural beings might originally have been described as "messengers" from God, they later became "mighty ones," "holy ones," "host of heaven," and even "divine beings." Sometimes cryptic names were used such as seraphim, cherubim, and ophannim.

In the Book of Daniel, some angels are even given personal names, such as Michael and Gabriel. Some of the Books of the Apocrypha (writings that were not canonized into the Bible) have a richer angelology.

Daniel claimed that Gabriel helped him interpret some of his visions. Certainly, without divine inspiration Daniel would not have been able to explain the dreams of King Nebuchadnezzer. The king demanded of his astrologers, who were wise men and magicians, that they interpret his dream, but he refused to tell them what his dream was. Only Daniel could come forth with the dream and its meaning.

210

THE FEAST OF TABERNACLES

... 'Go forth unto the mount, and fetch olive branches, and branches of wild olive, and myrtle branches, and palm branches, and branches of thick trees, to make booths, as it is written.'

Nehemiah 8:15

Israel: 1950
New Year Set Esrog and Lulov

IN the older biblical books, Sukkot, the Feast of Tabernacles, emerges as the festival that received the most attention, and it is speculated that it may have been the main festival of the Jews. It is clear that a similar festival observing the autumnal harvest was also previously celebrated by the Canaanites. Just how the etrog (citron) and lulov (the branch of palm leaves with sprigs of myrtle and willow twigs) came to be used in a ritual that required holding them and shaking and pointing them in all directions, is unclear. There was an old custom that dates to the time of the Second Temple which involved willow branches. Using willow branches, the observers of the custom beat the ground alongside the altar. This was probably an expression of fertility wishes for the coming year.

The four species are often seen as symbolic of different kinds of Jews. The citron has both taste and aroma and represents those Jews who do good deeds and also have knowledge of the Torah. The palm (date) has taste, but no aroma; the myrtle has aroma but not taste; and the willow has neither taste nor aroma. Each represents thereby, another group according to their knowledge of Torah and doing of good deeds.

THE SUKKAH

Israel: 1948
Emergency Stamps
Avraham Mapu's Sukkah

So the people went forth, and
brought them, and made
themselves booths, everyone
upon the roof of his house, and
in their courts, and in the courts
of the house of God, and in the
broad place of the water gate,
and in the broad place of the gate
of Ephraim.

Nehemiah 8:16

WHILE the Sukkot holiday is specifically tied to the construction of, and dwelling in, booths, as is mentioned in Nehemiah, scholars are not agreed that the Sukkah is a reminder of the exodus from Egypt and the living in tents while wandering through the wilderness. There is speculation that the Sukkah was taken from pagan ritual and Judaized. However, the Sukkah became an important feature of the celebration of the festival, particularly for Jews removed from the Palestine autumn harvest.

Pictured on this label, which was issued by the Jewish National Fund for fund-raising and educational purposes, is the Sukkah of Abraham Mapu. This label, along with many others, was pressed into emergency postal service in 1948 when the new State of Israel was born but postage stamps had not yet been printed. As with many "emergency stamps" it is not listed in the standard stamp catalogs (Scott). Mosden, a specialist's catalog, lists them for Israel.

Abraham Mapu was a teacher and writer who became

intensely interested in the Zionist movement. He expressed his ideas in a novel called *Love of Zion* which spread the influence of Zionism as it was translated from Lithuanian into English, French, Russian, Yiddish, Ladino, and Arabic. His influence on the early movement was so great that an Israel stamp in his memory was published in 1968.

EZRA AND
NEHEMIAH

Israel: 1970
20-Year's Anniversary
of Immigration of Jews from
Iraq

*. . . and the joy of Jerusalem
was heard even afar off.*

Nehemiah 12:43

THE design of this Israeli stamp features a symbolic representation of a dove flying towards the sun. The body of the dove is built of the Hebrew words "the immigration of Ezra and Nehemiah." The biblical reference is to the exodus from Babylonia to the land of Judah led by Ezra and Nehemiah where the rebuilding of Judaism and Jerusalem was carried out under their leadership.

The exodus of nearly 125,000 Iraqi Jews to Israel is commemorated in this stamp. Rioting against them by their Moslem neighbors in 1941, touched off the emigration of many Jews from Iraq, although they had to do so illegally. After the State of Israel was established, a legalization of the exodus of Jews who were willing to renounce their Iraqi citizenship was ultimately permitted by Iraq for a short period. While some Jews chose to remain even though many had acquired weapons as tensions between Jew and Moslem rose, there was a mass exodus. The Israeli government chartered airplanes to carry the Iraqi to their new-old homeland, Israel. The project was called "Operation Ezra and Nehemiah."

214

THE KINGS OF JUDAH

And Solomon's *son was*
Rehoboam; Abijah his son, Asa
his son, Jehoshaphat *his son;*
Joram his son, Ahaziah his son,
Joash his son; Amaziah his son,
Azariah his son, Jotham his son;
Ahaz his son, Hezekiah his son,
Manasseh *his son; Amon his son,*
Josiah *his son.*

Spain: 1962

I Chronicles 3:10-14

Patio of the Kings of Israel

ADORNING the façade of the El Escorial Monastery located near Madrid are six large statues of kings of Judah who contributed to the splendor or restoration of the Temple in Jerusalem. Eighteen feet tall, each statue stands on an inscribed pedestal which describes that particular king's major contribution to Temple life. The kings of Judah so honored are David, Solomon, Jehoshaphat, Hezekiah, Manasseh, and Josiah. Starting with King David, son succeeded father to the throne of Judah for seventeen generations, of which King Josiah was the last of the dynasty. (There is even a possibility that Shallum/ Jehoahaz was the son of Josiah, and thereby the dynasty was eighteen generations.)

The monastary was founded in honor of St. Laurence (San Lorenzo) to mark a victory of Spanish troops, against the French which occurred on that saint's day. San Lorenzo was martyred by being burned alive on a

215

gridiron and so the Monasterio De San Lorenzo El Real De El Escorial is designed in the shape of a gridiron. It was founded in 1563, less than one hundred years after the expulsion of the Jews from Spain. It is interesting that it was during the same century the Jewish kings were given so honored a place. The area in front of the church (as is the stamp also) is designated as the Patio of the Kings.

DAVID— KING OF ISRAEL

Hungary: 1970
King David on Throne
A Miniature Philatelic
Sheet from
Old Manuscripts

*And David reigned over all
Israel; and he executed justice
and righteousness unto all his people.*

I Chronicles 18:14

THE final book of the Hebrew Bible is a history of events from the creation to the end of the Babylonian exile. The Hebrew name of the Book of Chronicles translated is "events of the days." The Greek name is altogether different as it is translated as "concerning things omitted." Indeed, so as to condense the biblical books from Genesis through the Book of Kings, much had to be omitted. However, Chronicles is consistent in its omissions. It is written in such a way so as to emphasize the position of King David in Jewish history. David is presented in a glorified way, as is the House of David. Also the Temple and details of worship are extensively described. Events and information not found in earlier biblical books are also added (hence the Greek name for Chronicles), which further underscores the importance of King David and the Temple.

On this miniature philatelic sheet from Hungary, illustrations from old manuscripts are shown. The stamp in the lower right quadrant depicts King David seated on his throne. These stamps are semi-postals. An additional charge was added to the postal rate so as to raise funds for a welfare or civic project.

THIS is not the end. A book of this sort cannot end. Each year more stamps pour forth with designs that are based on biblical motifs. It cannot be otherwise. A book that has carried the message of ethical monotheism to all the parts of the world will continue to inspire idealists. A book that embodies such wisdom and beauty will continue to capture the philosophers and poets amongst us. The lovers of folklore and historians cannot find a greater treasure so well kept and so readily available. The prophetic message that teaches peace among peoples and concern for others will continue to have relevance always.

> They shall not hurt nor destroy in all my holy mountain; for the earth shall be full of the knowledge of the Lord, as the waters cover the sea.
>
> Isaiah 11:9

A Bibliography for the Beginning Stamp Enthusiast

The BAPIP Bulletin, a journal published by The British Association of Palestine-Israel Philatelists, Edgeware, Middlesex, England.

BLUMKIN, HELENE LAND, *Highlights of Jewish History on Israeli Stamps* (a monograph published originally as the "Pictorial Album" section of the *Congregation Kehilath Jeshurun 1956-1957 Yearbook*) (New York, New York).

The Coros Chronicle, a journal published bi-monthly by the Society of Collectors of Religion on Stamps. (Editor: Walter Sager; Los Angeles, California)

DAGONI, S. AND A. LINDENBAUM, *Judaica Guide for Stamp Collectors,* a brochure published under the auspices of the Haifa Philatelic Society, Haifa, Israel, 1963.

The Holy Land and Middle East Philatelic Magazine, a journal published monthly in London, England (Editor: E. Moshi).

The Holy Land Philatelist, a journal published monthly by Israeli Periodicals, Tel Aviv, Israel. (Ed., F.W.Pollack) (No longer pub.)

The Israel Philatelist, a journal published by the Society of Israel Philatelists (Editor: B. Adlerblum; Oak Park, Ill.).

The Judaica Philatelic Journal, a journal published quarterly by the Judaica Historical Philatelic Society (Editor: Maurice Burnston; Brooklyn, New York).

The Judaica Post, a journal published by Judaica Associates (Editor: Eli Grad; Detroit, Michigan). (No longer being published)

KAUFMAN, LEO AND BERL LOCKER, *The First Stamps of Israel,* a monograph published by the Government of Israel, Department of Posts, Telegraphs, and Telephones, Philatelic Services,1948.

LINDENBAUM, ARIEH, *Great Jews in Stamps* (Sabra Books: New York, New York, 1970).

Linn's Weekly Stamp News, a periodical published weekly for the general collector (Editor: George Linn; Sidney, Ohio) [See particularly Vol. 36, No. 11, whole number 1801]

LIVNI, ISRAEL, *Livni's Encyclopedia of Israel Stamps* (Tel Aviv, Israel: Sifrayat Ma'ariv, 1969).

Mosden Israel Catalogue (Editor: E. Mosden) (New York, New York: Middle East Stamp Co., 1970).

Philatelic Literature Review, a journal of the American Philatelic Research Library, Volume 19, Number 2 (Second Series Number 67), 1970 Second Quarter (State College, Pennsylvania).

WEITZ, EMIL, *A Glimpse into Jewish History Through Philately* (New York, New York: Israel Coin Distributors Corp., 1970).

220

A Bibliography for Readers Who Are Interested in More Information on People and Events Discussed in this Book

(BEITH), HAY, IAN, *Malta Epic* (New York: Appleton-Century Co., 1943).

BETTAN, ISRAEL, *The Five Scrolls* (Cincinnati: Union of American Hebrew Congregations, 1950).

BEWER, JULIUS, *The Prophets* (New York: Harper & Row, 1955).

BRADFORD, ERNGLE, *The Great Siege* (New York: Harcourt, Brace Co., 1962).

COHEN, A., the Rev., Dr. (editor), *The Five Megilloth* (London: The Soncino Press, 1965).

———— *Proverbs* (London: The Soncino Press, 1962).

———— (editor), *The Soncino Chumash* (London: The Soncino Press, 1956).

COMINS, HARRY L., *The Jewish Prophets* (New York: U.A.H.C., 1936).

DESLANDRES, YVONNE, *Delacroix* (N.Y. The Viking Press, 1963)

EISELEN, FREDERICK, E. LEWIS and D. DOWNEY (editors), *The Abingdon Bible Commentary* (New York: Abingdon-Cokesbury Press, 1929).

FREEHOF, SOLOMON B., *The Book of Job* (New York: U.A.H.C., 1958).

———— *Preface to Scripture* (New York: U.A.H.C., 1950).

GAER, JOSEPH, *The Lore of the Old Testament* (Boston: Little, Brown & Co., 1952).

GASTER, THEODOR, *Myth, Legends and Custom in the Old Testament* (New York: Harper & Row, 1969).

GINZBERG, LOUIS, *Legends of the Bible* (New York: Simon & Schuster, 1956).

GOODMAN, PHILLIP, *The Purim Anthology* (Philadelphia: The Jewish Publication Society of America, 1952).

HALL, MANLEY P., *The Secret Teachings of All Ages* (Los Angeles: The Philosophical Research Society, Inc., 1967).

HARRELSON, WALTER, *Interpreting the Old Testament* (New York: Holt, Rhinehart, & Winston, 1964).

HASTINGS, JAMES (editor), *Dictionary of the Bible* (New York: Chas. Scribner's Sons, 1963; Revised Edition).

HEIDAL, ALEXANDER, *The Gilgamesh Epic and Old Testament Parallels* (Chicago: Univ. of Chicago Press, 1963).

HERTZ, JOSEPH H., *Authorized Daily Prayer Book with Commentary* (New York: Bloch Publ. Co., 1960).

HERTZ, JOSEPH H. (editor), *The Pentateuch and Haftorahs* (London: The Soncino Press, 1952).

HONOR, LEO L., *Book of Kings* (New York: U.A.H.C., 1955).

KAUFMAN, LEO and LOCKER, BERL, *The First Stamps of Israel* (a monograph published by the Government of Israel) (Israel: Dept. of Posts, Telegraphs, and Telephones, Philatelic Services, 1948).

LAMSA, GEORGE, *Old Testament Light* (Englewood Cliffs, New Jersey, 1957).

LANDSBERGER, FRANZ (trans. Felix Gerson), *Rembrandt, The Jews and the Bible* (Philadelphia: Jewish Publication Society of America, 1946).

LIVNI, ISRAEL, *Livni's Encyclopedia of Israel Stamps* (Tel Aviv: Sifriat Ma'ariv, 1969).

MAXWELL, WILLIAM STIRLING, *Stories of the Spanish Artists Until Goya* (New York: Tudor Pub. Co., 1938).

NORTH, ERIC M., *The Book of a Thousand Tongues* (New York: Harper & Row, 1938).

SCHAUSS, HAYYIM, *The Jewish Festivals* (New York: U.A.H.C., 1938).

——, *The Lifetime of a Jew* (Cincinnati: U.A.H.C., 1950).

SCHWARTZMAN, SYLVAN D. and JACK SPIRO, *The Living Bible* (New York: U.A.H.C., 1962).

Scott's Standard Postage Stamp Catalogue (combined) (New York: Scott Publishing Co., 1971).

SEBEOK, THOMAS, *Myth: A Symposium* (Bloomington, Ind.: Indiana Univ. Press, 1971).

An Explanation as to How to Identify and Locate the Stamps Used in this Book

Almost all the postage stamps ever issued anywhere in the world are indexed in one or another catalogue. The best known of these for the American collector is the *Scott's Standard Postage Stamp Catalogue*. This catalogue, which has been exhaustively organized and compiled by many experts, is now over a hundred years old. An indication of its worth is that it is often called the "American Stamp Collector's Bible."

Therefore, wherever possible, the Scott identification number is given. To find any stamp, a collector needs only the country of origin and the Scott number. Other information, such as the year of issue, is helpful but not essential.

Certain stamps Scott refuses to list in the *Standard Catalogue*. Among these are the so-called "black blot" issues, which have really not been printed for postal use, but rather to exploit the stamp collector's interest in certain topics such as Art on Stamps, Religion on Stamps, Space Stamps, etc. These stamps Scott has listed in a separate catalogue, with the title *For the. Record*.

Stamps that are listed in the Scott Catalogue will be identified by their Scott number. Stamps which are unlisted (found in *For The Record*) will be identified by an asterisk (*). Where stamps are grouped together in pairs or more, on a given page, the listing reads from left to right, and from top to bottom for the proper numerical sequences.

One other catalogue is mentioned. Some stamps are rarely seen by the ordinary collector, and are of interest primarily for collectors who specialize in a given field. One such specialized catalogue is the *Mosden Israel Catalogue*. It lists all philatelic materials relating to Israel, including labels which have been converted to postal use, variations in color printing and perforation, etc., that interest the specialized Israel collector. Scott does not give the kind of profuse detail on these varieties and errors as do the specialized catalogues, therefore Mosden, Simon, Yvert and other such catalogues are recommended for the advanced Israel collectors.

CATALOGUE NUMBER INDEX

Unless otherwise indicated, all catalogue numbers are from
Scott's Standard Postage Stamp Catalogue.

PAGE NO.	COUNTRY	SCOTT NO.	PAGE NO.	COUNTRY	SCOTT NO.	PAGE NO.	COUNTRY	SCOTT NO.
1	United States	1371	60	Israel	106	115	Australia	307
2	Israel	298	61	Israel	108	116	Israel	184
3	Israel	299	63	Israel	114	117	Israel	185
4	Israel	300	64	Israel	111	119	Malta	340
5	Israel	301	65	Israel	112	120	Liberia	491
6	Israel	302	66	Israel	110	121	Israel	122
7	Israel	303	67	Israel	116	122	Israel	399
8	United States	1107	68	United Arab	8	123	Hungary	1947
9	Italy	830,831		Republic		124	Ajman	*
10	Belgium	549,550	69	United Arab	161,	126	Israel	186
11	Ajman	*		Republic 159, 160		127	Liberia	495
12	Yemen	*	71	Brazil	902	128	Yemen	*
13	Maldive Islands	297	72	Columbia	778	129	Lebanon	137
14	Vatican City	492	73	Israel	C23	130	Yemen	*
15	Vatican City	493	75	Israel	178	132	Israel	347
17	Aiman	*	76	Belgium	60-65	134	Israel	138
18	Fujeira	*	78	Portugal	1016	135	Ethiopia	415
19	Ajman	*	79	Israel	93	136	Yemen	*
20	Poland	1709	81	Israel	322	137	Yemen	*
21	Ajman	*	82	Paraguay	*	138	Yemen	*
23	Grenada	369	83	Czechoslovakia	1229	139	Yemen	*
24	Ajman	*	84	Arabian State of	*	140	Yemen	*
25	Maldive Islands	296		Upper Yafa		141	Abyssinia	87
26	Ajman	*	86	Spain	1561	142	Columbia	C504
27	Togo	646	88	Israel	149	143	Vatican City	C3, C7
28	Iceland	278	89	United States	627,	145	Vatican City	388
29	Israel	394			657	146	United Nations	177,
30	Israel	395	90	Israel	102		178, Hungary	1462
31	Israel	396	91	Israel	87	147	Israel	72
32	Armenia	293	92	Israel	267	148	Italy	818
33	Israel	397	93	Switzerland	B383	149	Israel	225, 226
34	Vatican City	C6	94	United States	924	150	Israel	227
35	Italy	638	95	New Zealand	408	151	Israel	123
36	Israel	398	96	Israel	348	152	Israel	79
37	Trinidad and	185	97	Israel	220	153	Czechoslovakia	1476
	Tobago		99	Israel	145-148	156	Israel	295
38	St. Helena	101	100A	Israel	162-164	157	Israel	352
39	St. Helena	103	101	Israel	33	158	Israel	346
40	Yugoslavia	1037	102	Israel	267	159	Israel	141
42	Spain	922	103	Israel	346	160	Israel	374
44	Rwandi	212	104	Israel	107	161	Surinam	360
45	Arabian State of	*	106	Israel	115	162	Israel	372
	Oman		107	Israel	113	163	Israel	373
47	Yugoslavia	1039	108	Israel	109	164	Vatican City	390
49	Spain	1160	109	Surinam	359	166	Italy	825
50	Surinam	361	110	Czechoslovakia	45	167	Israel	353, 354
51	France	1054		(Bohemia and		168	Arabian State of	*
53	Spain	1344		Moravia)			Oman	
54	Palestine	73	111	Israel	208	170	Italy	826
55	Hungary	2023	112	Hungary	2024	171	Israel	237
56	Israel	105-116	113	Spain	1343	172	Brazil	872
58	Israel	105	114	Israel	173	173	Italy	816

PAGE NO.	COUNTRY	SCOTT NO.	PAGE NO.	COUNTRY	SCOTT NO.	PAGE NO.	COUNTRY	SCOTT NO.
174	Vatican City	391	18	Israel	364	202	Rwandia	214, 218
175	Israel	144	190	Israel	367	204	Israel	69, 68, 67, 66
176	Italy	824	191	Israel	101	206	Romania	1912
177	Israel	243	192	Grenada	332, 331,	208	Grenada	323
178	Israel	244			334, 329	209	Italy	820
179	Israel	242	194	Israel	371	210	Portugal	883
180	Russia	2305	195	Israel	103, 121	211	Israel	35
181	Israel	179	196	Israel	100	212	Israel-Mosden	T.30
182	Israel	35	197	Israel	351	214	Israel	424
184	Brazil	988	198	Israel	350	215	Spain	1021
185	Italy	823	199	Israel	349	217	Hungary	283
186	Israel	12	200	Israel	139			
187	Israel	221	201	Israel	140			

INDEX

Aaron, 93
Abel, 22
Abraham, 35, 40, 42, 62, 87
Abraham's Sacrifice (Benković), 40
Abyssinia, 62
Adam, 9, 13, 16, 20-21, 23-24, 86, 118
Adam (Dürer), 11
Adam (Rodin), 13, 25
Adam and Eve (Cranach), 19
Adam and Eve (Titian), 23
Aden, 74
Ahaz, 148
Ajman, 11, 17, 19, 21, 24, 26, 124
Aleijadinho, 172
Amalekites, 92
Ammonites, 116
Amos (Prophet), 175
Amsterdam, 125
Ancient musical instruments of Israel, 195
Apollo 8 Space Flight, 1
Apollo XI Moonshot, 192-193
Arch of Titus (Rome), 79, 90
Armenia, 32
Ascensión (Island of), 39
Asher, 65-66, 105
Ashera (deity), 65
Assyria, 148
Assyro-Babylonian Mythology, 4, 15
Aswan Dam, 69
Audacity (Sert), 113
Australia, 115

Babylonian Exile, 147, 170
Balaam, 94
Balak, 94
Balfour, Lord Arthur James, 167

Balfour Declaration, 167
Bath-sheba, 123-124
Bath-sheba (Rembrandt), 124
Bath-sheba at Her Bath (Ricci), 123
Belgium, 10, 76
Belshazzar's Feast (Rembrandt), 208
Belvoir Castle, 115
Benjamin, 60, 67
Benkovic, Federico, 40
Berne, Switzerland, 93
Beth Shearim, 200
Bible, 95, 100, 115, 124, 148-149, 159, 180, 194-195, 209, *passim*
Bilhah, 58, 63, 66
BILU, 147
Bohemia, 110
Brazil, 71, 172, 184
British Mandate, 200
Budapest Museum of Fine Arts, 123
Buddha, 127
Budweis, 110

Cain, 21
Calebites, 61
Cana, Alonso, 86
Canaan, Canaanites, 61, 65, 92, 111, 160, 211
Caravaggio, Polidoro da, 120
Chagall, Marc, 122
Chaldea, 176
China, 127
Christ, 176
Christmas, 3
Chronicles, Book of, 217
Church of Bom Jesus do Matosinhos, 172
Churchill, Winston, 193

226

Circumcision (Cana), 86
Columbia, 72
Cranach, Lucas, 19
Creation (Michelangelo), 2-7, 9-10, 14-15, 18, 26-27, 145, 148, 164, 166, 170, 173-174, 176, 185, 209
Cyprus, 101
Czechoslovakia, 83, 110, 153

Dan, 60, 66, 105, 108
Daniel (Prophet), 168-169, 208-210
Daniel, Book of, 84, 208-210
Darwin, Charles, 6
David, 41, 62, 117-120, 122-124, 126, 130, 160, 215, 217-218
David and Goliath (Caravaggio), 120
Dead Sea, 152
Decalogue, the, 78, 130
Declaration of Independence, 89
Delacroix, Eugène, 51
Delilah, 110
Deuteronomy, Book of, 57, 82, 95, *passim*
Dinah, 60
Druze, 73
Dürer, Albrecht, 11
Dutch Guiana, 50, 109, 161

Ecclesiastes, Book of, 198
Eden, 150
Edom, Edomites, 46, 61
Egypt, 68-69, 106, 158, 165
El Escorial, 215-216
Elhanan, 120
Eliezer (servant of Abraham), 42, 44
Elijah, 41, 72
Ephraim, 57, 106
Esau, 45-46
Esther, 206-207
Ethiopia, 62
Eve, 9, 13, 15-16, 18, 20, 23-24, 26
Eve (Rodin), 25
Exodus (ship), 92
Exodus, the, 182
Expo 1970 (Japan), 23
Ezekiel (Prophet), 170-171, 175, 198
Ezra, 214

Flinck, Govert, 46
France, 51
Fujeira, 18

briel, 126, 210

Gad, 64, 66, 105
Ganges River, 41
Garden of Eden, 20, 27
Genesis, Book of, 2, 4-6, 10, 16, 57-58, 60, 66, *passim*
Gersoniden, 153
Ghent, 17
Gibeah, 67
Gilgal, 116
Gilgamesh, 29-30, 32
Giorgione, 127
God, 6-8, 20-23, 34-36, 40-41, 43, 48, 76, 91-94, 100, 102, 117, 124-125, 145, 148, 157, 174, 176-177, 179, 191, 194, 199, 205
Goliath, 119-120
Gomorrah, 42,43, 203
Grenada, Grenadines, 23, 192-193, 208

Habakkuk (Prophet), 175
Hagar, 66
Haggai (Prophet), 175
Haifa, 92
Halle Bridge, 41
Halley, Edmund, 2
Haman, 206
Heliodorus Driven from the Temple (Delacroix), 51
Herod, 130
Heroes and Martyrs Day, 97, 187
Hezekiah, 145, 215
Hitler, Adolf, 187-188, 190
Hobab, 74
Holy Ark, the, 130-131, 160
Hooghly Bridge, 41
Horites, 66
Hosea (Prophet), 175
Hungary, 55, 112, 123, 146, 217-218
Hyksos, 68

Iceland, 28
Immanuel, 148
Independence Hall (Phila.), 89
India, 41, 179
International Geophysical Year, 8
Iraq, 214
Isaac, 40-42, 45
Isaac Blessing Jacob (Flinck), 46
Isaiah (Prophet), 145-150, 175, 180-181
Ishbi-benob, 120
Ishmael, 66
Ishtar (deity), 207

Israel, 2-7, 22, 29-31, 33, 36, 56, 58, 60-61, 63-67, 72-75, 79-82, 88-92, 96-104, 106-108, 111, 114, 116-117, 121-122, 126, 131, 145, 147-152, 154, 156-160, 163, 167, 171, 175, 177-179, 181-182, 186-191, 194-201, 204-205, 212, 214.
Israel, Northern Kingdom of, 175
Issachar, 105, 107
Italy, 9, 148, 166, 170, 173, 209
IXOYE, 176

Jaare-oregim, 120
Jabesh, 116
Jacob, 44-51, 53-54, 56-58, 60-61, 63-64, 66-67, 106-108
Jacob's Flock (Ribera), 49
Jacob's Ladder (Zefarovic), 47
Jacob Wrestling with the Angel (Delacroix), 51
Jacob Wrestling with the Angel (Sert), 53
Jalkut Shimeoni, 12
Jebusites, 160
Jehoahaz, 215
Jehoshophat, 215
Jerahmeelites, 61
Jeremiah (Prophet), 164-166, 170, 175, 198
Jeremiah Lamenting the Destruction of Jerusalem (Rembrandt), 168
Jericho, 191
Jerusalem, 117, 126, 130-131, 151, 158, 160, 162-163, 168, 170, 181, 185, 215
Jethro, 73-74
Jewish National Fund, 212
Job, 203, 205
Job, Book of, 198, 202-203
Joel (Prophet), 172-173
Jonah (Prophet), 175-179
Jonah, Book of, 177-178
Jonathan ben Shimea, 120
Jordan River, 64
Joseph, 55, 57, 68, 106
Joseph Explaining a Dream (Langetti), 55
Josephus, Flavius, 38
Joshua, 66
Joshua, Book of, 60, 66
Josiah, 215
Judah, 60-62, 105
Judah, Southern Kingdom of, 61, 175, 215

Judah Maccabee, 130
Judea, 148
Judges, Book of, 67

Kalderon, Asher, 126
Kenites, 61
Kidron River, 38
King David (Chagall), 122
King James Version, 148
Korah, 187

Laban, 50, 54
Lachmi, 120
Langetti, Giovanni, 55
Leah, 60, 63, 107
Lebanon, 128
Levi, 60, 104-105
Leviticus, Book of, 89, *passim*
Liberia, 120, 127
Liberty Bell (Phila.), 89
Lilith, 15-16
Lisboa, Antonio, 172
Lodz, Poland, 183
London Times, 182
Lot, 38-39
Lot's Wife (geog. formation), 38
Love of Zion (Mapu), 213

Maderuelo, 24
Maimonides, 53
Major Prophets, the, 175
Malachi (Prophet), 175
Maldive Islands, 13
Malta, 119
Manasseh (Patriarch), 57, 64, 106
Manasseh (King), 215
Maori Bible, 95
Mauritius, 101
Mapu, Abraham, 212-213
Marduk (deity), 207
Maximilian I, Emperor, 11
Medes, 208
Menelik I, 62
Messiah, 41, 62, 124
Methuseleh, 36
Micah (Prophet), 175, 180-181
Michael, 210
Michelangelo, 8-9, 14, 18, 26-27, 82-84, 145, 148, 164, 166, 170, 173-174, 176, 185, 209
Midianites, 61, 73
Minor Prophets, the, 175
Moab, 94

Montefiore, Moses, 163
Montpellier, France, 115
Moravia, 110
Mordecai, 206-207
Moresheth-Gath, 181
Morse, Samuel F. B., 94
Moses, 35, 41, 57, 73-74, 78, 82-85,
  87, 91, 93, 96, 98, 107-108, 187
Moses (Michelangelo), 82, 84
Moslems, 12
Mount Ararat, 32
Mount Sinai, 78, 87
Mount Vesivius, 38
Murillo, Bartolomé Esteban, 42-44

Nahor, 66
Nahum (Prophet), 175, 184
Nahum, Book of, 184
Nahum (Lisboa), 184
Naphtali, 66, 105
Napoleon Bonaparte, 39
Nasser, Gamal, 103
Nathan (Prophet), 123
Nebi Shu'aib, 73
Nebuchadnezzar, 168-169, 185, 210
Nehemiah, 214
Nehemiah, Book of, 212
New Guinea, 179
New Testament, 196
New Zealand, 95
Nile River, 69
Nineveh, 177, 184
Noah, 29, 32, 35-37, 87
Numbers, Book of, 57, 94, *passim*
Nuremburg, 11

Obadiah (Prophet), 175
Oman, 168
"Operation Don Quixote," 163
"Operation Ezra and Nehemiah," 214
"Operation Magic Carpet," 75
Ottoman Empire, 152

Palestine, 54, 101, 167, 200, 212
Paradise, 15
Paraguay, 82
Passover, 160, 182
Persians, 208
Pharaoh, 68, 106
Philadelphia, Pa., 89
Philistines, 111, 113
Pliny, 33
Plutarch, 121

Poland, 20
Pompeii, 38
Portugal, 78, 210
Portuguese Inquisition, 161
Proverbs, Book of, 5, 197-199, 201
Psalms, Book of, 5, 187, 193-194, 196

Quarim, 15
Queen of Sheba, 62

Rachel, 44, 54, 63, 66-67, 106-107
Ramses II, 69
Rappaport, Nathan, 189
Rebecca at the Well (Murillo), 42-44
Rembrandt van Rijn, 124-125, 168, 20(
  208
Reuben, 58-59, 64, 105
Reuel, 74
Reynolds, Sir Joshua, 115
Ricci, Sebastiano, 123
Rocca, Michel, 112
Rodin, Auguste, 13, 25
Roman Empire, 114
Romania, 206
Rosh Hashana, 191
Rwandi, 43-44, 202

Sabbath, 35, 87, 201
Sadducees, 190
St. Helena, 38-39
St Laurence (San Lorenzo), 215
St. Michael and the Dragon (Delacroix),
  51
Saint Sulpice, 51-52
Samson, 110-113
Samson and Delilah (Rocca), 112
Samuel, 115-116
Satan, 191
Saul, 116, 126
Savannah, Surinam, 161
Sephardim, 151
Sert, José, 53, 113
Shakespeare, William, 123
Shallum, 215
Shechem, 60
Shiloh, 67
Sibbecai, 120
Simeon, 57, 60, 105
Sistine Chapel, 8-9
Six Day War (1967), 103, 131, 158
Sodom, 42,43, 203
Solomon, 62, 126, 128-130, 205, 215
Song of Deborah, 57, 66

Song of Songs (Canticles), 204-205
Soviet Union, 146, 153
Spain, 42-43, 49, 86, 113, 215-216
Stjorn, 28
Stone of Scone, 47
Straits of Tiran, 103, 158
Suez Canal, 158
Sukkot, 212-212
Suleiman the Magnificent, 119
Surinam, 50, 109, 161
Switzerland, 93
Syria, 49, 148
Szyk, Arthur, 182-183

Tabernacle, the, 79
Talmud, 14
Taluth, 116
Tate Gallery (London), 115
Temple, the, 41, 48, 79, 81, 90, 126, 129-131, 160, 166, 168, 170, 185, 211, 215, 218
Ten Commandments (see Decalogue)
The Babylonian Job, 202
The Gathering and Eating of Manna (Vasquez), 72
The Infant Samuel (Reynolds), 115
The Judgment of Solomon (Giorgione), 127
"The Twelve," 175
Thomson, Stith, 128
Titian, 23
Tobago, 37
Togo, 27
Torah, 96, 157, 196-197, 199, 211
Tree of Knowledge, 18, 20
Tree of Life, 12, 20
Trinidad, 37
Twelve Tribes of Israel, 56-67, 104-105

United Arab Republic, 69

United Nations, 13, 88, 146, 155, 171
United Nations Plaza (N.Y.C.), 146
United States, 1, 8, 89, 94
Universal Declaration of Human Rights, 13
University of Copenhagen, 28
Upper Volta, 84
Uriah, 123
Urim and Thummim, 104-105
Utnapishtim, 29-30, 32
Uzziah, 145

Van der Goes, Hugo, 17
Vasquez, 72
Vatican, 14-15, 34, 145, 164, 173
Vishnu, 176
Vitebsk, Russia, 122

Warsaw Ghetto, 188-189
Weizman, Chaim, 94, 167
Westminster Abbey, 47
White House, the, 183
Windesi, 179
Windward Islands, 192
Wisdom Literature, 198

Xisuthros, 30, 32

Yemen, 12, 74, 128, 130-131
Yom T'ruah, 191
Yugoslavia, 40, 47

Zahal, 103
Zebulon, 63, 105
Zechariah (Prophet), 175, 185-186
Zefarovic, Hristofer, 47
Zilpah, 63
Zipporah, 73
Zim, Yaakov, 190
Zionism, 147, 153-154
Ziusudra, 30